D0437457

POWER DIVIDED IS POWER CHECKED

POWER DIVIDED IS POWER CHECKED

THE ARGUMENT FOR STATES' RIGHTS

JASON LEWIS

BASCOM HILL PUBLISHING GROUP

MINNEAPOLIS, MN

COPYRIGHT © 2011 BY JASON LEWIS.

BASCOM HILL
PUBLISHING GROUP

BASCOM HILL PUBLISHING GROUP
212 3ᴿᴰ AVENUE NORTH, SUITE 290
MINNEAPOLIS, MN 55401
612.455.2293
WWW.BASCOMHILLPUBLISHING.COM

ALL RIGHTS RESERVED. NO PART OF THIS PUBLICATION MAY BE REPRODUCED,
STORED IN A RETRIEVAL SYSTEM, OR TRANSMITTED, IN ANY FORM OR BY
ANY MEANS, ELECTRONIC, MECHANICAL, PHOTOCOPYING, RECORDING, OR
OTHERWISE, WITHOUT THE PRIOR WRITTEN PERMISSION OF THE AUTHOR.

ISBN : 978-1-935098-50-8
LCCN: 2010913745

PRINTED IN THE UNITED STATES OF AMERICA

"The powers delegated by the proposed Constitution to the federal government are few and defined. Those which are to remain in the state governments are numerous and indefinite... The powers reserved to the several states will extend to all the objects which, in the course of ordinary affairs, concern the lives, liberties, and properties of the people, and the internal order, improvement, and prosperity of the state."

~James Madison, "Federalist 45"

For my mother and father,

who introduced me to the world of politics

at an early age (often against my will),

and for my wife and children,

for whom I have tried to do the same.

ACKNOWLEDGEMENTS

MY SINCERE THANKS to Mark Levine and Bascom Hill Publishing Group for taking on this topic. I've felt strongly about this issue for years and appreciate their willingness to put my views in print. I also thank my editor, Marly Cornell, for her fastidious workmanship in reviewing my manuscript.

Of course, I thank all those scholars who have done the vital research that I found both invaluable and inspiring. They are referenced in the book so I won't name them here, but they laid the foundation upon which my work, and that of so many others, is based.

Thanks also to my radio producer, Brendan Kearin, who picked up the slack at the office while I was busy with the book.

Last, but certainly not least, I am indebted to my family for putting up with the many hours I spent away from them, laboring in what they call my "bat cave." They are my inspiration.

CONTENTS

FOREWORD

I LISTEN REGULARLY to Jason Lewis's radio show because of his cogent, well-prepared insights that you won't hear anyplace else. For anyone who has heard Jason on his national radio show, listened to him when he substituted for Rush Limbaugh, or read his opinion pieces in places such as the *Wall Street Journal*, you know what I am talking about. This book is a genuine treat. The book continues Jason's trademark style by providing a real education, in this case on why "states' rights" has been so important to America's success and why the nationalization of decisions threatens American's freedom.

This book couldn't be more timely. With the federal government quickly taking over ever more aspects of our lives, the last vestiges of individual choice seem to be disappearing. Local citizens, who know to pick the rules that best serve their interests, instead face thousands of federal criminal statutes governing everything from the size of your toilet tank, the water pressure in your shower, and what your children can study in school. One of the remarkable benefits of the American experiment is that permitting states to make decisions in the past has allowed Americans to learn from the mistakes of others.

In the past, if states that made bad decisions were unwilling to reconsider them, Americans had the ability to move to other states. If healthcare regulations lowered the quality of healthcare, and raised costs enough, Americans could move to a state with more acceptable options. We are quickly losing not only this important way of evaluating laws, but we have also lost our freedom to move away from bad government decisions.

Jason Lewis has the rare knack for putting ideas across in a jargon-free commonsense way. This concise and carefully written book provides the highlights of the legal history of the relationship between the states and the federal government. And he takes on the hard issues in a way that is thoughtful, not ideological.

America has moved far from the constitutional protections that were originally set up to protect freedom.

Jason not only explains where we are and how we got here; he also offers a way out of the constitutional malaise the nation finds itself in today. If his viewpoint seems radical, it's only because we have drifted so far from the limited government tradition that the author attempts to reclaim.

Read this book and you'll have a much greater understanding of just how fragile the republic has become. You will also, assuming Lewis' prescription is followed, have much-needed hope for the future.

John Lott, PhD, economist and senior research scientist at University of Maryland, and author of five books including *Freedomnomics, The Bias Against Guns, and More Guns, Less Crime*

INTRODUCTION

FOR TOO LONG, the concept of "states' rights" has had a negative connotation. Racial strife in the post-Civil War era made taboo the notion of returning power to the states. But allocating power to the several states was never about race; it was about a constitutional framework that hoped to limit the mistakes of government and provide the greatest amount of freedom and decision-making to the people in the several states. Rediscovering the principles of dividing power within the republic is the best guarantor that the errors of the past don't return on a much larger scale.

At the end of the first decade of the twenty-first century, we are a divided nation—precisely because we have chosen to consolidate government by unleashing it from its constitutional moorings. A one-size-fits-all policy dictated by unelected bureaucrats and judges in Washington D.C.

has not brought the country together—to the contrary, it has torn us apart. For example, three of the most divisive issues of our time will not be decided by the people, but most likely by the Supreme Court of the United States.

The citizens of Arizona, facing fiscal and social upheaval, decided to restore the rule of law to their state's border. Arizona's elected representatives sensibly voted to codify federal immigration policy under their inherent authority to police the law—only to find that a federal court, at the behest of the Justice Department, rejected the legislation. The judge went so far as to suggest that Arizona's enforcement of immigration law would place an impermissible burden on federal authorities.[1] The state be damned.

In California, a federal judge overruled the express will of the voters as reflected in Proposition 8, which had defined marriage in the Golden State as between a man and a woman.[2] The opinion was a fanciful case of legal reasoning that somehow found a constitutional right to same-sex unions, even though, as Chapter Five notes, marriage and family law has long been the province of the states. If the highest court in the land eventually upholds the decision, it will redefine the institution of marriage (for good or ill) for the entire country, not just California.

Finally, the fate of American healthcare, how we get it and how much, will also lie in the hands of the federal judiciary. The constitutionality of "Obamacare"—specifically, the mandate that all Americans must purchase a government-approved health plan—has been challenged by a number of states. And they have been given the green light to take the case forward.[3] Here's one possible reason: the so-called "fine" for refusing to purchase health insurance amounts to an unconstitutional direct tax on the average citizen. That is, there is no taxable event that would trigger an indirect tax, such as the case with an excise tax. No, the president's plan taxes you if you *don't* do something.

The common thread in all three issues is the rise of a federal behemoth overwhelming the states and their citizens. Frankly, it matters less what side of the issue you're on and more on whether you'll have a meaningful say in the debate. If most of America feels frustrated, that's why.

In fact, states' rights is the elephant in the living room. What powers do the several states retain? Can we return to a constitutional framework envisioned by the framers? Or has the federal government permanently usurped the framers intent? And what would actually happen if one state decided to test the boundaries of Washington?

This book examines the constitutional and legal history from the framers to the Civil War, to the New Deal, and through the Warren Court. And after outlining the convoluted legal history that has unfortunately brought America to this constitutional precipice, I present a call to action with a new constitutional amendment designed to restore the fundamental tenants of federalism. As part of this new amendment, I ask every American to support an energetic reaffirmation of local control that allows for any state to peaceably leave the union (barring all other remedies of which the text outlines) thus providing the ultimate check on federal intrusion—and, in the process, helping to preserve the most effective constitutional design for freedom itself.

INTRODUCTION NOTES

1. http://www.azcentral.com/ic/pdf/0729sb1070-bolton-ruling.pdf (Accessed July 2010)

2. http://www.sfgate.com/cgi-bin/article.cgi?f=/c/a/2010/08/04/MNQS1EOR3D. DTL (Accessed July 2010)

3. http://www.bbc.co.uk/news/world-us-canada-10847519?print=true (Accessed July 2010)

CHAPTER 1

Lincoln's Dilemma or How We Got Here, and Where We're Headed

IT IS AN OBVIOUS UNDERSTATEMENT to say the Civil War changed America. A nation divided, whose wounds spilled blood and treasure from North to South. The country would never be the same—but not for the reasons most people think.

While slavery was mercifully conquered, animosities between generations of Americans lingered well into the twentieth century. More important, the War Between the States, as it came to be known, irretrievably altered the nation's constitutional framework—and *not* for the better. As one political commentator succinctly put it, "The long-term result of the Civil War was to make the federal government an irresistible force. The states were crushed—not only the Southern states, but finally the power of all the states to withstand federal tyranny."[1]

As much as anything, the North's willingness to go to war over the issue of secession was what fundamentally transformed the relationship between the federal government and the individual states. Indeed, had the war been only about freeing the slaves, nonviolent solutions were possibly within reach. The idea of "emancipated compensation" had been debated all the way back to the founding.[2] Critics of Abraham Lincoln, such as Professor Thomas DiLorenzo of Loyola, suggest that the option of "peaceful" emancipation prior to bloodshed was unwisely rejected by the sixteenth president.[3] Late into the war, Lincoln reportedly presented to his cabinet the idea of compensating slave holders as a condition of the South's surrender, but the cabinet rejected the idea.[4]

Though we can't conclusively know whether war over slavery could have been avoided, there were other issues of paramount importance that led to the conflict between North and South, and eventually secession. In fact, Southern displeasure toward national policy was evident at the earliest points of our nation's history.

Alexander Hamilton's 1790 plan for a national bank, for instance, generally favored the North by assuming the States' Revolutionary War debt.[5] But it was federal protectionism designed to preserve the North's manufacturing base that had long been an irritant simmering in the South. When Lincoln moved to raise tariffs on those Southern states that were heavily reliant on imports, he reopened an economic wound that went all the way back to the "tariffs of abominations" in 1828.[6]

The power to collect these duties, by force if necessary, was absolute in Lincoln's mind. That was hardly surprising, given that protectionism was a hallmark for Republican politics at the time.[7] The levies, however, had the effect of converting even ardent nationalists like John Calhoun of South Carolina into "nullification" advocates due to what they described as the "'tyranny' of the Northern majority which had imposed the tariff."[8] Secession was in the air.

Far from treasonous, as DiLorenzo points out, secession was long considered the ultimate safety valve against federal encroachment.[9] The right of states to voluntarily leave the Union had been debated at the Constitutional Convention, and the notion of a permanent compact rejected.[10] In short, the framers had to answer the fundamental question that all governments must eventually address: should relations between fellow citizens be voluntary? For those seeking self-government, the answer was obvious.

In the early days, the New England federalists seriously contemplated secession over the Louisiana Purchase and what they considered to be Thomas Jefferson's attempts at weakening Northern power.[11] Abolitionists such as John Quincy Adams had proclaimed that if "states shall be alienated from each other" it is better to "part in friendship from each other, than to be held together by constraint."[12] And even before the first shot was fired on Fort Sumter, there was still "widespread sentiment in the North in favor of allowing the Southern states to peacefully secede."[13]

Lincoln held very different views. He declared the "Union is perpetual" and through the sheer force of personality had successfully convinced enough of the electorate that "no state, upon its own mere motion, can lawfully get out of the Union."[14] He had also assured the South that he would not interfere with slavery; after all, the abolitionist movement was still relatively small and the North had its own history of discrimination.[15] Secession became an easier issue to sell because so many in the North were simply not willing to fight over the issue of emancipation alone.[16]

In fact, Union commander Gen. George B. McClellan once predicted that Northern soldiers would mutiny if they knew their efforts were specifically aimed at emancipating blacks.[17] General William Tecumsch Sherman, the man responsible for the bloody march across the South, had little time for abolitionists, no real problem with slavery, and considered his years living in Charleston to be some of his best. But he valued the Union more and wouldn't tolerate secession.[18]

Of course, slavery was still of paramount importance to constituents of the Deep South who greatly feared Northern talk that encouraged insurrection. But they, too, thought the institution of slavery was secure because the federal government had no legal authority to effectively end it should the Southern states secede. On the eve of Lincoln's inauguration, President James Buchanan conceded there was no federal power to force a state to remain in the Union, declaring "that our Union rests upon public opinion, and can never be cemented by the blood of its citizens shed in a civil war..."[19]

Nevertheless, President Lincoln framed the conflict in secessionist terms. And he now faced a Hobson's choice— either preserve the constitutional design as it was written, or preserve the Union at a staggering cost.[20] Lincoln chose the latter, but "saving the Union" cost 600,000 lives in America's bloodiest and most divisive conflict. The prosecution of the war also resulted in the suspension of the writ of habeas corpus, martial law, the restriction of freedom of the press (including the jailing of Northerners deemed as possibly sympathetic to the Confederacy), and more military tribunals by far than any other administration. None of which conclusively suggests the war should not have been fought. However, more than just a few of Lincoln's most vehement critics have questioned why the Founding Fathers are routinely vilified over their silence on slavery, while the sixteenth president is revered for exploiting the issue when the war actually had more to do with secession.[21]

In any event, the North's determination to go to war, and the South's reaction to it, helped to diminish the idea of "states' rights" for at least the next century. The very notion itself became a pejorative one. Unfortunately, federalism—or what the framers intended the relationship between the central government and the states to look like—was also a casualty. The framers' goal was "a compound republic" that would divide the government "into distinct and separate departments" and "guard one part of the society against the injustice of the other part."[22]

The aftermath of the Civil War ushered in a brave new world, resulting in a consolidation of power in Washington that would have been unthinkable at the founding. Though America is far removed from the issues of the nineteenth century, the federal government's reach is larger and more powerful than ever. But, at long last, a backlash may finally be brewing.

So-called "Tea Party" protests were spontaneously formed in 2009 to counter what became the most ambitious federal bailout in history, dubbed the Troubled Asset Relief Program, or TARP. Opponents deride it as a $700 billion unlawful appropriation, essentially transferring legislative authority to the Treasury Department. Citing well-established principles of separation of powers, the critics note that "Congress may not delegate its lawmaking authority to the executive branch."[23]

That's not all. Federal pay czars, forced bankruptcies, and private sector shakedowns, not to mention massive increases in federal spending in the so-called "economic stimulus" bills, reawakened a silent majority. And the inexorable drive towards federal control of healthcare—especially the requirement in the 2010 overhaul that Americans purchase individual health insurance—is starting to profoundly shift the electoral landscape.

(Republican Senator Scott Brown's upset victory in Massachusetts being another example.)

Indeed, the issue of federal intrusion has become so big that the newly elected governor of Virginia, Bob McDonnell, said, "I think you're going to see a resurgence of discussions of federalism, about the Tenth Amendment, about limits on federal power, and federal spending."[24]

A resurgence is already in evidence. Limited government activists are demanding that political parties adopt a clear stand against "a federal government that is too big, too intrusive, and all too eager to seize power from the states."[25] State legislatures are fighting back, passing bills or proposing constitutional amendments that prohibit Washington from imposing new mandates. A number of states have even passed so-called "sovereignty measures" designed to reinvigorate what President Ronald Reagan called the "new federalism."[26] Tennessee and Montana want to exempt their citizens' firearms from federal law, and Texas Governor Rick Perry even mentioned the "s" word, suggesting that Washington's thirst for power could lead a few states beyond "sovereignty" resolutions to actual secession.[27]

The Supreme Court in *Printz* ruled that the federal legislature may not "command the states' executive power" (by requiring, in that case, state officials to conduct background checks of weapons purchases pursuant to the Brady Handgun Violence Prevention Act.), but Congress continues to find creative ways to dictate state policy.[28] Extension of unemployment compensation and increased Medicaid reimbursements, for instance, cost the states billions, as funding for these programs is shared between federal and state governments. Yet, if states increase their commitments toward the programs, there is no guarantee Washington won't cut off federal dollars in the future, leaving local government to shoulder the entire cost. The same is true for many transportation initiatives, such as mass transit, under the federal highway trust fund.

As a result, there seems to be little doubt that this federal micromanaging of the most arcane pieces of state law has exhausted the patience of state legislators.[29] "Why would I want to rule anything out?" asked Rep. Charles Key of Oklahoma. "Why would we take a position that says, 'We really don't like this but we're only going to go so far?'"[30] This sounds like a nation getting close to the tipping point.

Too many of our leaders have simply forgotten what our republic was supposed to look like. American government rests upon the horizontal checks and balances we read about in civics classes. But our republic's most important (and undervalued) characteristic is the vertical separation of powers as described by the framers. Dual sovereignty between the federal government and the states ensures a strict division of power. It is not only the best guarantor of liberty, but remains "the true theory" of our Constitution.[31] "The way to have good and safe government," according to Thomas Jefferson, "is not to trust it all to one, but to divide it among the many."[32] Later in his autobiography, the "Sage of Monticello" offered this as well: "It's not by the consolidation or concentration of powers, but by their distribution that good government is effected. Were it not this great country already divided into states, that division must be made..."[33]

In other words: power divided is power checked.

Here the federal judiciary could play a constructive role within its proper sphere by striking down legislation that is clearly beyond the expressed constitutional powers of the federal government. Instead, they seem to have aided and abetted federal expansion, while at the same time severely curtailing the constitutional prerogative of the states. That is, activist judges have stretched the constitutional limits of central power while simultaneously imposing their will on the states—and not just on the hot button issues of abortion or the death penalty, but on routine matters of state law governing term limits, religious displays, welfare requirements, family law (including marriage), and criminal justice. The federal courts have even taken over local school districts.[34]

Yet this form of judicial supremacy was never supposed to occur. "Of the three powers," in the words of Montesquieu (from whom much of the separation of powers doctrine originates), "the judiciary is next to nothing."[35] For good reason. As Justice Felix Frankfurter once warned, "…if the people in the distribution of powers under the Constitution should ever think of making judges supreme arbiters in political controversies, they will dethrone themselves" and create a power "more dangerous than the worst elective oligarchy in the worst of times."[36]

Alas, in 1803 the Supreme Court struck down the Judiciary Act of 1789, effectively establishing judicial review.[37] The decision was controversial and the federal courts remained wary of settling most local disputes right into the twentieth century. "The Courts," according to constitutional historian, Forrest McDonald, "were not expressly given the power to rule on constitutionality. The nearest thing to a direct statement on the subject is the supreme law clause."[38] Jefferson remained a leading skeptic, thinking judicial review imperious and often describing the Court's rulings as anti-republican. In 1820 he wrote, "I know no safe depository of the ultimate powers of the society but the people themselves..."[39] Fellow Virginian John Randolph also denied such plenary power to the judiciary, asking, "Are we not as deeply interested in the true exposition of the Constitution as the judges can be? Is not Congress capable of self-government?"[40]

Federalists such as Madison were also worried about the separation of powers, wondering "upon what principle it can be contended that any one department draws from the Constitution greater powers than another in making out the limits of the powers of the several departments."[41] None of them contemplated the federal courts dictating policy to the states.

It is worth remembering that the Constitution was not written to protect us from one another; it was written to protect the states and the people from a newly created central government—about which many of the founders had understandable reservations given their colonial experience—an experience that led to, well, secession.

"The two enemies of the people are criminals and government," Jefferson declared, "so let us tie the second down with the chains of the Constitution so the second will not become the first."[42] The three fundamental threats to individual liberty come from foreign enemies, domestic crime, and government. The framers believed that the federal government would handle the first; the states would govern the second, and the Constitution the third.

In matters of crime, the colonists wished to avoid the dangers of a nationalized police force, one of the hallmarks of a totalitarian regime. Hence, the power of the *polis* (commonly referred to as the police power or the "inherent and plenary power of a sovereign to make all laws necessary and proper to preserve the public security, order, health, morality, and justice.") was reserved for state governments that existed long before constitutional ratification.[43] By delegating matters of war and peace to the newly formed central government, the framers merely confirmed the arrangement. After all, the states had created the national government; they were not about to give up their sovereign powers over internal disputes involving their own citizens residing within a particular state.

To be sure, the delegates at the Constitutional Convention did spell out those things that were to be prohibited to the states, and they also granted the federal government judicial power for those "controversies between two or more states" and "between citizens of different states."[44] But as Madison (known as the Father of the Constitution) would reiterate, the "proposed government cannot be deemed a national one, since its jurisdiction extends to certain enumerated objects only, and leaves to the several states a residuary and inviolable sovereignty over all other objects."[45]

Even Alexander Hamilton, long considered the champion of an energetic central government, confirmed that political power would be "divided between the national and state governments" so that "each of the portions of powers delegated to the one or to the other...is...sovereign with regard to its proper objects.[46] These were to be the cornerstones of the new republic: a "government of law and not of men," where the limited powers of central authority were specifically enumerated.[47]

On this, the Tenth Amendment to the Constitution is clear: The powers not delegated to the United States by the Constitution, nor prohibited by it to the states, are reserved to the states respectively, or to the people.

Nonetheless, modern-day activists have successfully convinced the courts, as well as the American people, that subsequent amendments to the document, in particular the

Fourteenth, altered the entire constitutional framework bequeathed to us by those who ratified it. The effect has rendered the Tenth Amendment essentially dormant, leaving the states and the people at the whim of an unlimited central authority. A dangerous proposition, considering that "in framing a government which is to be administered by men over men, the great difficulty lies in this: you must first enable the government to control the governed; and in the next place oblige it to control itself."[48]

Well, the federal government hasn't had much difficulty in controlling the governed lately, but it has had great difficulty in controlling itself. This is not only contrary to the framers' intent, but a serious threat to our individual freedoms. The Declaration of Independence recognized that governments exist only "to secure these rights" and would only derive "their just powers from the consent of the governed."[49] Americans don't seem too eager to consent to a federal behemoth that only a few generations ago would have been unrecognizable.

The Declaration, of course, also warns "that governments long established...not be changed for light or transient causes."[50] But as Jefferson saw it, "whenever any form of government becomes destructive" to these unalienable rights, "it is the right of the people to alter or to abolish it..."[51]

The federal government has overstepped its bounds. And the effect has been to polarize the nation over the most contentious issues of the day that would be far better settled at the state level. One byproduct has been fiercely partisan fights over Supreme Court nominees due to the ill-advised power bequeathed to the modern judiciary. Subsequent chapters describe how the American experiment of limited, constitutional government has come under attack from those who should be protecting it and, barring a change in course, what a free people should consider doing about it.

CHAPTER 1 NOTES

1. Joseph Sobran, "Restore the Constitution," *Chronicles*, October 2000, 14.

2. Joseph Ellis, *Founding Brothers* (New York: Alfred Knopf, 2000) 92. Gouverneur Morris, constitutional delegate from Pennsylvania had "proposed a national tax to compensate the slave owners," suggesting that would be preferable than to "saddle posterity such a Constitution."

3. Thomas J. DiLorenzo, *The Real Lincoln* (Roseville, CA: Prima Publishing, 2002) 48-50.

4. Jay Winik, *April 1865* (New York: Harper Collins, 2001) 34.

5. Ellis, *Founding Brothers*, 57, 58. Many of the Southern states had less debt, had already paid it off, or sold it to speculators.

6. Edwin C. Rozwenc, *The Making of An American Society*, (Boston: Allyn and Bacon, 1972) 414.

7. DiLorenzo, *The Real Lincoln,* 73.

8. Rozwenc, *The Making*, "Nullification" being the mechanism by which states could simply ignore federal law.

9. DiLorenzo, *The Real Lincoln*

10. Winik, *April 1865*, Though one of the youngest delegates, Charles Pickney of South Carolina was influential, but his proposal that "the Union shall be perpetual" was never considered.

11. Forrest McDonald, *States' Rights and the Union*, (Lawrence: University Press of Kansas, 2000) 59. "Jefferson had doubts about the constitutionally of the purchase" and had drafted "an amendment to that end." His doubts were eventually eased by none other than Thomas Paine who argued that it made "no alteration in the Constitution."

12. DiLorenzo, *The Real Lincoln*, 88.

13. Ibid., 101. According to Thomas DiLorenzo, "Maryland's political leaders favored peaceful secession" and feared, as did others, "that forcing a state at gunpoint to remain a part of the Union would destroy the concept of the Union as a voluntary association of states..."

14. Roy P. Basler, *Collected Works of Abraham Lincoln*, Abraham Lincoln Online: Speeches and Writings, http://showcase.netins.net/web/creative/lincoln/speeches/1inaug.htm (Accessed January 2010)

15. DiLorenzo, *The Real Lincoln*, 236. "So-called Black Codes existed in the North decades before such discriminatory laws were enacted in the South after Reconstruction."

16. Tucker Bowen, producer/director/writer, LINCOLN: AMERICAN MASTERMIND, National Geographic Television Channel, 2009.

17. Edward C. Smith, "The Civil War Series: 1864 would prove pivotal to conflict's outcome," *The Washington Times*, 6 February 1999, B3.

18. Winik, *April 1865*, 305.

19. Rozwenc, *The Making*, 541, 542.

20. DiLorenzo, *The Real Lincoln*, 48-50.

21. Ellis, *Founding Brothers*, 83-88, 89, 90. Even though Jefferson's initial draft of the Declaration had strongly criticized the slave trade, and the Constitution allowed for its interrupting in 1808, the founders' first concern was establishing the Union. Nearly all the founders, as we've come to define them, were philosophically opposed to the institution, if not entirely willing to give it up. Ellis notes their "egalitarian principles" helped to place slavery on "the permanent defensive." Benjamin Franklin had endorsed a Quaker abolitionist petition, and Jefferson himself had endorsed emancipation in his *Notes on the State of Virginia* as well as, in 1784, proposing a bill in Congress to prohibit slavery in the western territories. It failed by one vote. Though wishful thinking at the time, there was "a prevailing consensus that slavery was already on the road to extinction."

22. James Madison, "Federalist 51," *The Federalist Papers*, edited by Michael L. Chadwick, (Washington: Global Affairs Publishing Co., 1987) 283.

23. The Troubled Asset Recovery Program or TARP. *Freedom Works Foundation, No. 124*, "Constitutional Infirmities in the EESA of 2008," 13 January 2009.

24. Brendan Miniter, "Back to Basics GOP," *The Wall Street Journal*, 2 January 2010, A9.

25. Stephanie Simon, "Colorado GOP Writes Its Own Invitation to the Tea Party," *The Wall Street Journal*, 1 December 2009.

26. Dinesh D'Souza, *Ronald Reagan, How an Ordinary Man Became an Extraordinary Leader* (New York: Touchstone, 1997) 263.

27. Kathy Kiely, *USA Today*, 15 May 2009.

28. *Printz v. United States*, 521 U.S. 898, 1997.

29. Extension of unemployment compensation as well as increased Medicaid funding cost the states billions, as funding for these programs is shared between federal and state governments. But if states increase their commitments toward the programs, there is no guarantee Washington won't cut off funding in the future, leaving local government to shoulder the entire cost. The same is true for many transportation initiatives, such as mass transit, under the federal highway trust fund.

30. Kiely, *USA Today*

31. http://etext.virginia.edu/jefferson/quotations/ jeff1050.htm (Accessed February 2010) Jefferson to Gideon Granger, 1800, ME. 10:168. "The true theory of our Constitution is surely the wisest and best, that the states are independent as to everything within themselves, and united as to everything respecting foreign nations."

32. http://etext.virginia.edu/jefferson/quotations/ jeff1050.htm (Accessed December 2009) Jefferson to Joseph C. Cabell, 1816, ME. 14:421. 1821, ME 1:12,

33. Ibid.

34. http://www.cato.org/pubs/pas/pa-298.html (Accessed November 2009) "In 1985 a federal district judge took partial control over the troubled Kansas City, Missouri, School District (KCMSD) on the grounds that it was an unconstitutionally segregated district with dilapidated facilities, and students who performed poorly. In an effort to bring the district into compliance with his liberal interpretation of federal law, the judge ordered the state and district to spend nearly two billion dollars over the next twelve years to build new schools, integrate classrooms, and bring student test scores up to national norms." None of which had the desired effect. The District began closing a number of schools.

35. Baron de Montesquieu, *Spirit of the Laws*, 1748.

36. Clarence Manion, *Cancer in the Constitution*, (Shepherdsville: Victor Publishing Co., 1972) 5, 6. Frankfurter, quoting from a previous Court in *Baker v Carr*, which established the so-called "one man, one vote" rule used to intervene in a Tennessee case surrounding the apportionment for state house seats by its own legislature. Historically these political matters had been left to the elected branches of government per Article 1, Section 4 of the Constitution. See Chapter Seven for more.

37. See *Marbury v. Madison* 5 U.S. 137 (1803).

38. Forrest McDonald, *Novus Ordo Seclorum* (Lawrence: University Press of Kansas, 1985) 255.

39. Thomas Jefferson to William C. Jarvis, 1820. ME 15:278. http://etext.virginia.edu/ jefferson/quotations/jeff0500.htm (Accessed March 2010)

40. Rozwenc, *The Making,* 277.

41. Lance Banning, *The Sacred Fire of Liberty: James Madison and the Founding of the Federal Republic* (Ithaca: Cornell University Press, 1995) *278.*

42. http://wiki.monticello.org/mediawiki/index.php (Accessed March 2010)

43. Bryan A. Garner, *Black's Law Dictionary, 7th Edition* (St. Paul: West Group, 1999) 1178.

44. See the *Constitution of the United States*, Article III, Section 2.

45. Madison, "Federalist 39," *The Federalist Papers*, 207.

46. McDonald, *Novus Ordo Seclorum*, 278.

47. Rozwenc, *The Making,* 201. John Adams, primary author of the Massachusetts Constitution of 1780, called for a distinct separation of power between branches so as "to end that it may be a government of laws and not of men."

48. Madison, "Federalist 51," 281.

49. See *The Declaration of Independence*, Philadelphia: July 4, 1776.

50. Ibid.

51. Ibid.

CHAPTER 2

Don't Make a Federal Case Out of It

IF THERE'S A POSTER CHILD for Washington micromanaging, it might just be the Environmental Protection Agency. Businessmen and women under the iron fist of this green bureaucracy must surely wonder just how the planet survived prior to President Nixon's creation of the Agency in 1970. The air and water have been improving for decades, but the EPA's relentless intrusion only seems to grow.[1] That's one reason for Governor Perry's ire. While the EPA has put Texas in the federal agency's crosshairs, citing an insufficient pollution permitting process, the state points to a twenty-two percent drop in ozone between 2000 and 2008.[2] This detail has fallen on deaf ears.

Of course this is not just about Texas or ozone. In California, the U.S. Fish and Wildlife Service has nearly bankrupted agriculture in the San Joaquin Valley as a result of their "biological opinion," protecting the delta smelt by diverting massive amounts of water to the ocean.[3] Though the tiny creature is found only in California, it was somehow awarded interstate protection under the Endangered Species Act.

The mother of all federal mandates is undoubtedly the EPA's "endangerment finding" on so-called greenhouse gases. At the behest of a minority of states, the Supreme Court overturned a lower court opinion by ruling, under the Clean Air Act of 1970, that the EPA has the power to regulate carbon dioxide as a pollutant, though the "greenhouse gas" was never contemplated as a pollutant when the law was passed.[4]

Consequently, the Agency is now set to implement the most sweeping regulations in United States history, imposing drastic energy limits upon the states by dictating all manners of fuel efficiency on their residents—even down to the kind of light bulbs they may use.[5] If Congress passes similar legislation, such as the American Clean Energy and Security Act, the costs for energy consumers have been estimated at nearly a trillion dollars.[6] States are so fearful of the regulations that a number of them, including Texas and Virginia, are devising ways to challenge the EPA's authority to dictate such a policy on carbon dioxide.

The sad lesson is this: by granting arbitrary enforcement powers to a myriad of federal agencies, the government has turned the average citizen into an environmental criminal. Hysteria over so-called "environmental tobacco smoke," for example, led Congress to pass the Family Smoking Prevention and Tobacco Control Act, thus granting the Food and Drug Administration power to control personal smoking habits.[7] "The antithesis of the rule of law," as one observer wryly noted, "is not anarchy, but a tyranny of laws."[8]

The federal green brigade seems incapable of understanding the positive correlation between a nation's wealth and a cleaner environment. As an economy grows, it can afford more regulations and associated costs. Of course the inverse is true as well. If you want to stifle economic growth, slapping on more and more rules does the trick. That's one reason why China and India were so vehemently opposed to the drastic global warming regulations pushed by activists at the failed climate summit in Copenhagen in 2009. These are the activists that we now know included the very United Nations panel that member countries rely on for their public policy data.[9]

Where this will end is anyone's guess. After all, if one assumes that most pollution is, by definition, interstate, the same theoretical rationale for federal regulations would inevitably lead to some form of global governance—unless you believe the evils of pollution obey national borders. The environmental endgame, and what seems desirable by so many green advocates, is global enforcement. American sovereignty may be in the proverbial crosshairs.

Environmentalism is certainly one of the most pronounced federal intrusions into our daily lives, but far from the only one. The 2008 Federal Register, which documents all federal regulations, has now reached almost 80,000 pages according to the Competitive Enterprise Institute.[10] Regulatory costs are now over one trillion dollars annually, and "the annual outflow of roughly 4,000 final rules has meant that well over 40,000 final rules were issued during the past decade."[11] The federal tax code alone now totals over nine million words, ten times more than the Holy Bible.[12] Compliance costs are now estimated to be near $300 billion annually, above and beyond an estimated $1.5 trillion in federal taxes paid.[13]

Criminal justice is also getting into the act. Though the Constitution mentions only three federal crimes, "Congress has enacted over 4,000 federal crimes."[14] They cover everything from the "air you breathe, the water you drink, the size of your toilet tank, the water pressure in your shower, the words you can speak under oath and in private, how your physician treats your illness, what your children study in grade school, how fast you can drive your car, and what you can drink before you drive it are all regulated by federal law."[15] Under the 1,000-page, $33 billion, 1994 Crime Bill, the majority of crimes involving a firearm have effectively become federal offenses.[16]

Former Attorney General Edwin Meese is fond of saying, "Let's not make a federal case out of it," but that is exactly what we have done.[17] Our new national motto more closely resembles "There ought to be a law." An American Bar Association task force that Meese chaired in 1999, as well as a similar report authored by Chief Justice William Rehnquist the year before, warned of the dangers of "duplicative prosecutions at the state and federal levels for the same course of conduct," i.e., double jeopardy.[18] That is much less a problem when federal prosecutions are restricted to only those cases where there is an enumerated federal interest.

The problem became so acute by the late 1990s that "forty percent of the federal criminal provisions enacted since the Civil War became law in just the last three decades."[19] And one reason, according to Messrs. Meese and Rehnquist, is Congressional grandstanding when it comes to high-profile media cases.

Consider the tragic affair of Terri Schiavo in 2005. The press coverage of a helpless women's plight was, to say the least, heartrending. Who would advocate for a disabled woman whose life was being jeopardized by a detached husband who had already moved on with his life and whose zeal to pull her feeding tube bordered on the obsessive? Certainly a fair question. And yet, through years of litigation (and against the wishes of her parents) the courts of justice in Florida refused to intervene and stop what was, according to her husband (the legal guardian), a previously stated desire to end her own life.

So Congress did. By granting special legislation giving the federal courts the task of reviewing Terri Schiavo's tragic predicament, politicians from both sides of the aisle actually weakened the life support system for the republic. The ability to regulate behavior between citizens of the same state has always resided with the several states, for good or ill.

Proponents of the Schiavo intervention would exploit the same vehicle that big-government liberals used to override state law: the "due process" clause of the Fourteenth Amendment, which prohibits any state from depriving "any person of life, liberty, or property, without due process of law; nor deny to any person within its jurisdiction the equal protection of the laws," and, as we shall see, has been the source of so much federal mischief.[20] There are, no doubt, procedural restrictions on what states may do when prosecuting criminal defendants, but the law itself was to remain with the states. Proponents in Congress (though they wanted to go much further) say the final legislation that passed with the president's last-minute signature was procedural in nature and was not a scrutinizing of the substance of the law, only the fairness of the hearings. In that regard, it was unlike the substantive "due process" litmus test used by activist courts to strike down actual state law.

But, as opponents of the legislation pointed out, "if Congress were authorized to reopen every state court decision involving a potential procedural due process claim...then there would be absolutely no finality to state court judgments in this country."[21] Even conservative judge Stanley F. Birch castigated Congress and the administration for overstepping its bounds by demanding a federal review of the case "in a manner squarely at odds with our Founding Fathers' blueprint."[22]

Terri Schiavo was being persecuted by her husband, not the state—to which the constitutional rights of habeas corpus and others are meant to apply. Michael Schiavo, not Terri, was in fact the <u>defendant</u> in the case because in the eyes of the plaintiffs, Terri Schiavo's parents, he was responsible for their daughter's rights being violated. So how could Congress or the federal courts assert a "due process" claim on behalf of a victim who was not a party to the litigation? For that and other reasons, the state court found that Florida family law was relatively clear on the issue of spousal rights in the absence of a written directive, and upheld the high standard for injunctive relief.

Many Americans believe (as do I) that what happened to Ms. Schiavo was simply wrong. But Congress has little, if any, role in such affairs. Family and criminal law involving state citizens has long been established as within the purview of the respective states, providing they don't have runaway courts. But there can hardly be a "due process" claim for the failure of the state legislature to sufficiently protect someone. If so, Congress and the federal courts will be telling the states which laws to pass for every circumstance. Look at it this way: had it been the wish of Terry Schiavo's parents to pull the tube, against that of her husband, it's likely the same court rulings would have saved her life. What we appear to have witnessed is a valid court decision, but based on bad state law.

There is a larger issue here: relying on federal judges who preside over a much larger territory runs the risk of doing for the country what one errant state judge may have done for Florida. That would threaten many more Terri Schiavos, not to mention our republican model of divided government. In the final analysis, it is the law in Florida that should be changed to protect innocent life in this circumstance, not the Constitution.[23]

It was simply not the framer's design to involve Congressional action in routine criminal cases, especially when previous avenues to the federal bench have been rebuffed.[24] In most murder cases, the defendant is charged by state authorities. That is as it should be if you're at all concerned about the consolidation of prosecutorial power. Article IV, Section 4, even requires an "application" by the states for federal protection as it pertains to domestic (not in the modern-day sense between spouses, but events within a nation) violence.[25] As Chief Justice John Marshall declared in *Cohens v. Virginia*, Congress simply does not possess the power to "punish murder committed within any of the states," and it is "clear that Congress cannot punish felonies generally."[26]

Marshall was merely following the wishes of Madison, et al., who had warned against a federal role for everything from religion to education to welfare, "in short, everything, from the highest object of state legislation down to the most minute object of the police."[27] That's why the federal government's judicial power extends to those limited cases where a diversity of parties exists that transcends state borders. In fact, preventing the concentration of power in a national authority is what distinguishes the American criminal justice system from a police state. Federalism has always been the *sine qua non* of limited government because it offers the only real safety valve from an overreaching government: the ability to flee.

Perhaps the document has been misinterpreted for so long that social conservatives are now willing to use it to the advantage of their own agenda. But after *Schiavo,* will it not be more difficult to express justifiable indignation at, say, the recent explosion of federal hate crimes statutes that were passed in honor of the late liberal lion, Senator Edward Kennedy?

The Matthew Shepard and James Byrd, Jr. Hate Crimes Prevention Act was signed into law by President Barack Obama as part of a defense appropriation bill in 2009.[28] The legislation's eponymous martyr was a gay University of Wyoming student murdered in a state without a hate crime statute on the books. Matthew Shepard thus became a national symbol for proponents of federal hate crime legislation.[29] Though many states already had such laws pertaining to assaults motivated by different kinds of malice (not just its intensity), Senator Kennedy led the Democratic effort to expand current federal law to include sexual orientation and gender.

But federal hate crime laws are no more justified than the Schiavo intervention was. And they raise disturbing questions about freedom of expression by attempting to judge state of mind, and not just prove it. Ironically, the same liberal who decries flag burning legislation on the grounds that burning a flag should not be judged on the basis of the underlying motive seems to have no hesitancy in doing the same for criminal behavior. What many fear next is prohibiting the thought or expression itself.

There is also the issue of equal justice when criminal punishment depends on the ethnicity or behavior of the victim, thus seeming to elevate the value of one life over another. The Georgia Supreme Court held that state's overly broad hate crime law unconstitutional precisely due to prison sentences that were greater "because of bias or prejudice."[30] And if empowering courts to judge the kinds of criminal malice isn't problematic enough, the idea of <u>federalizing the criminal code</u> is.[31]

Often, big-government advocates point to the supremacy clause as a facile justification for more federal law. It states that the "Constitution and the Laws of the United States which shall be made in pursuance thereof... shall be the Supreme Law of the Land..," but note the qualifier, *"in pursuance thereof..."*[32] *McColluch v. Maryland* helped to establish federal supremacy, but only when federal law is within its legitimate sphere.[33] During oral arguments in a case calling for the confinement of sexual predators, Justice Scalia was forthright when he stated, "There is no constitutional power on the part of the federal government to protect society from sexual predators."[34] Even the power to craft legislation that is "necessary and proper" is valid only when the law is "within the scope of the Constitution."[35] Perhaps the Constitution demands that principle should trump fear.

Let's remember that prosecutorial indiscretion from a central authority was something the British had employed to cower the colonists; consequently, the framers were fearful of a one size-fits-all criminal code bringing all Americans under the jurisdiction of a federal aristocracy. Jefferson had proclaimed that Congressional "acts which assume to create or define or punish crimes other than those so enumerated in the Constitution are altogether void and of no force."[36] Moreover, he declared, "The power to create, define, and punish such other crimes is reserved, and of right appertains solely and exclusively to the respective states, each within its own territory."[37]

Madison, Hamilton, and Jefferson, who held differing views on the new central government, were in agreement on how the states—and not the federal government—should protect their citizens from one another in most internal matters. Hamilton, the poster boy for a more energetic central government, declared that, "The administration of private justice between citizens of the same state...all those things, in short, which are proper to be provided for by local legislation, can never be desirable cares of a general jurisdiction." [38]

Madison proclaimed those powers "reserved to the several States will extend to all the objects which, in the ordinary course of affairs, concern the lives, liberties, and properties of the people, and the internal order, improvement, and prosperity of the State."[39]

The founders' belief in a central government with strictly limited jurisdiction reflects their colonial experience. That's why the Constitution is explicit on the matter. If the federal government were to have unlimited plenary power, there would hardly be a need for Article 1, Section 8, that specifically sets out legislative authority.[40] This view held sway well into the twentieth century before it came under attack.[41]

There have been a few recent exceptions where the high court thankfully toyed with the idea of limiting the concentration of power in Washington. Though little has changed the overall trend, in *Kimel* and *Garrett* the Court rediscovered the Eleventh Amendment—granting states "immunity not only from suits in federal court by outsiders, as the amendment expressly says, but also from suits by the federal government and by citizens of the states itself."[42]

The justices said that Fourteenth Amendment challenges to state regulations must rise to the level of the framers' intent to overrule state sovereignty. McDonald notes Justice Anthony M. Kennedy's majority opinion, saying, "Our federalism requires that Congress treat the states in a manner consistent with their status as residuary sovereigns and joint participants in the governance of the nation."[43] The fact that the rulings were greeted with such surprise was an indication of how far we have drifted from original intent.

Lopez and *Morrison*, a few years earlier, were also welcome if not brief attempts at restoring constitutional integrity. In *United States v. Morrison*, the Court held that Congress had no power to pass the 1994 Violence Against Women Act. Chief Justice Rehnquist reiterated that the Fourteenth Amendment allowed Congress to regulate state action only, not "the actions of private persons" in civil cases.[44] Citing the first tests of the Fourteenth Amendment in 1883, the chief justice's majority opinion endorsed "the enduring vitality of the Civil Rights Cases and *Harris*," which declared the amendment barred state discrimination, not that of private individuals.[45]

The majority was equally convincing in *United States v. Lopez*, writing that Congress had also overstepped its authority by regulating private actions of a non-economic nature.[46] As we shall see in a later chapter, however, the multitude of laws restricting private action remain firmly in place as long as they can somehow be tied to "commerce," no matter how inconsequential the economic activity might be "among the several states."[47] Because of this, and contrary to some legal handwringing at the time, these rulings were hardly sweeping in their effect.

CHAPTER 2 NOTES

1. See the Pacific Research Institute's annual *Index of Leading Environmental Indicators*, 14th edition (2009) http://liberty.pacificresearch.org/docLib/20090414_Env_Index_09.pdf. (Accessed January 2010)

2. Ana Campoy, "EPA Tangles with Texas in Battle Over Air Quality," *The Wall Street Journal*, 21 November 2009, A4. "Our results speak louder than bureaucratic meddling," was the quote from the governor's spokesperson, citing the drop in ozone.

3. "California's Man-Made Drought," *The Wall Street Journal*, 2 September 2009, www.opinionjournal.com (Accessed September 2009)

4. *Massachusetts v. Environmental Protection Agency*, 549 U.S. 497 (2007).

5. http://www.startribune.com/templates/fdcp?1268856099576 (Accessed June 2010) The 2007 Energy Independence and Security Act starts phasing out the incandescent light bulb in 2012 in favor of the "energy efficient" (and more expensive) compact fluorescent bulb. Local legislators say the federal law shouldn't apply to bulbs made and consumed in one state and have introduced state bills to that effect.

6. www.texaspolicy.com/pdf/2009-09-PP25-ACES-khw.pdf. (Accessed December 2009) Congressional Budget Office estimate cited by the Texas Public Policy Foundation, 2009.

7. Rita Rubin, "FDA Announces Tobacco Restrictions," *USA Today*, 19 March 2010

8. Robert J. Ernst, III, "*The Real Environmental Crisis: Environmental Law,*" Imprimis Vol. 23, No. 5, May 1994.

9. www.examiner.com/x-11224-Baltimore-Weather-Examiner~y2009m11d30-Climategate-Penn-State-Professor-Mann-under-investigation (Accessed March 2010) Global warming proponents at Britain's Climate Research Unit at the University of East Anglia as well as Penn State's Earth System Science Center have been investigated for activities surrounding manipulation of data and the peer review process included in the 2007 Intergovernmental Panel on Climate Change since 2009.

10. Clyde Wayne Crews, "Ten Thousand Commandments 2009," *Competitive Enterprise Institute*, http://cei.org/issue-analysis/2009/05/28/ten-thousand-commandments (Accessed January 2010)

11. Ibid.

12. Steve Forbes, *Flat Tax Revolution* (Washington: Regnery Publishing Inc., 2005).

13. See *Tax Foundation*, http://www.taxfoundation.org/research/show/1962.html. (Accessed January 2010)

14. Andrew Napolitano, "Most Presidents Ignore the Constitution," *The Wall Street Journal*, 29 October 2009.

15. Ibid.

16. "You Have the Right to Remain Funded," *Wall Street Journal*, 24 August 1994, A10.

17. Edwin Meese, III, "The Dangerous Federalization of Crime," *The Wall Street Journal*, 22 February 1999.

18. Ibid.

19. Ibid.

20. See Fourteenth Amendment to the United States Constitution, ratified 1868.

21. Opposition brief filed by Michael Schiavo, *Schiavo v. Schiavo*, (04A825) United States Supreme Court, 2005.

22. Stephen Henderson, "Conservative Judge Blasts Bush, Congress for Role in Schiavo Case," *Knight Ridder/Tribune Information Services*. 30 March 2005.

23. *Cruzan v. Director, Missouri Dept. of Health* 497 U.S. at 289 (J. O'Connor, concurring) Ironically, the Supreme Court has ruled that there is an inherent "liberty interest in refusing unwanted medical treatment...including the artificial delivery of food and water" may actually tie up such efforts at providing sustenance through state law.

24. Hamilton, "Federalist 81," *The Federalist Papers*, 439.In this way, federalism and separation of powers are the flip sides of the same coin. The Schiavo case had been previously appealed to the federal courts and denied, so may Congress act when the judiciary has not? As Hamilton said, "A legislature, without exceeding its province, cannot reverse a determination once made in a particular case, though it may prescribe a new rule for future cases."

25. See U.S. Constitution, Article IV, Section 4. 1787.

26. Edward Conrad Smith, *The Constitution of the United States with Case Summaries*, Tenth Edition, (New York: Harper Row, 1975) 99. That remains the case as there are only federal laws concerning the murder of government officials, not a general statute.

27. http://www.constitution.org/je/je4_cong_deb_12.htm. (Accessed February 2010) Madison, often referred to as the Father of the Constitution, in debate on the Cod Fishery Bill, granting bounties.

28. The Matthew Shepard and James Byrd, Jr. Hate Crimes Prevention Act. Public Law 111-84 National Defense Authorization Act for Fiscal Year 2010. National Archives and Records Administration.

29. *20/20*, ABC News Corp., November 26, 2004. According to *ABC News*, the
     Shepard murder may not have been solely a "hate crime," but a drug-related
     mugging gone bad, as well.

30. Bill Rankin, "Ruling Overturns State Hate Crime Law," *Atlanta Journal
     Constitution* 26 October 2004.(Accessed November 2009)

31. *Apprendi v. New Jersey* (99-478) 159 N.J. 7, 731 A. 2d 485, United States
     Supreme Court, 2000.The Supreme Court has upheld state "hate crime"
     legislation (See 1993's *Wisconsin v. Mitchell*) and, while it did not directly
     address a hate crime statute in *Apprendi v. New Jersey*, it did rule that
     enhancing a criminal sentence on the basis of a bias finding must be proved
     to a jury beyond a reasonable doubt. It also ruled that allowing a judge
     to increase a sentence on only a preponderance of evidence would be a
     violation of due process.

32. United States Constitution, Article VI, 1787.

33. Smith, *The Constitution, McColluch v. Maryland* (1819).

34. Review & Outlook, "Predators and the Constitution," *The Wall Street Journal*,
     19 January 2010, www.opinionjournal.com (Accessed February 2010).

35. Smith, *The Constitution, McColluch v. Maryland* (1819) 66, 67.

36. Thomas Jefferson, *Draft Kentucky Resolutions* "http://etext.lib.virginia.edu/
     jefferson/ quotations/index.html", 1798. ME 17:380, Charlottesville (VA):
     University of Virginia Library, Electronic Text Center; 1995; c1999. (Accessed
     January 2010)

37. Ibid.

38. Hamilton, "Federalist 17," *The Federalist Papers*, 86, 87.

39. Madison, "Federalist 45," *The Federalist Papers*, 252.

40. To be sure, the Constitution does explicitly grant federal power in Article 1, Section 8, but for only those items mentioned, such as bankruptcy law, patents, and regulating interstate commerce. See United States Constitution.

41. Smith, *The Constitution,* 101. Justice Louis Brandeis noted in the 1938 *Erie Railroad v. Tompkins* decision that matters not governed by the federal government were state concerns, and he even went on to say, "there is no federal general common law."

42. McDonald, *States' Rights,* 233. See *Kimel v. Florida Board of Regents 528 U.S. 62 (2000)* and *Board of Trustees of the University of Alabama v. Garrett, 531 U.S. 356 (2001).*

43. Ibid.

44. Rehnquist's majority opinion in *United States v. Morrison,* 529 U.S. 598 (2000).

45. Ibid. The Civil Rights Cases turned out to be historically prescient. During the era of Jim Crow, the real impediment to black progress lay in state-sponsored discrimination. A number of businesses wished to serve and employ blacks in the early twentieth century but were effectively barred from doing so by "legislation that forced the segregation of blacks and whites." As economist Don Boudreaux stated, "Jim Crow itself was government power." http://stossel.blogs.foxbusiness.com/2010/05/25/fire/-john-stossel/print/ (Accessed June 2010).

46. The Court struck down the Gun Free School Zone Act of 1990 as exceeding the federal government's power to regulate economic activity under the Commerce Clause. *United States v. Lopez,* 514 US 549 (1995).

47. *Heart of Atlanta Motel v. United States*, 379 U.S. 241 (1964). Traditionally there had been no federal protection for the infringement of civil rights in private affairs. Succinctly, the federal government was to prohibit state-sponsored discrimination via the Fourteenth Amendment, and the states were left to regulate the affairs between private individuals. But in *Heart of Atlanta Motel*, the Supreme Court upheld *federal* anti-discrimination laws pertaining to "public accommodations" as an extension of Congress' power to regulate interstate commerce, however "local," due to its "effect upon that commerce."

CHAPTER 3

Due Process

THE GENESIS OF OUR DEMOCRACY may have started with Greek and Roman law, but it was the Age of Enlightenment that really nourished the American Revolution. The idea that human rights exist independent of government set the foundation for most of the freedoms we now take for granted, such as a fair hearing before any tribunal. In theory, the Supreme Court itself has acknowledged these rights exist "by the law of the land long antecedent to the organization of the state, and can only be taken...by due process of law."[1]

Colonial charters reflected this view. Before the federal Bill of Rights, there was the Virginia Declaration of Rights in 1776. Shortly thereafter, Pennsylvania followed suit with its own proclamation. By the time of the Constitution's ratification, most of the states had their own Bill of Rights. Because of this, the Founding Fathers saw no need to look toward the new central government for the protection of their liberties. They had already secured them. Federalists actually argued against the federal Bill of Rights as a repetitious acknowledgment of English common law, dating back to the Magna Carta.[2]

It's not that Federalists were proponents of big government. Quite the contrary. A few historians may claim that Madison's support for states' rights while in Congress amounted to a grand reversal of some sort, but he was never the ardent nationalist revisionists made him out to be.[3] Madison's Virginia Plan, granting a legislative veto over state law, was aimed at protecting states from one another and securing the "general government's supremacy within in a system where the overwhelming burden of political responsibilities would still be carried by the states."[4] He had initially expressed concern over a federal Bill of Rights because "by enumerating particular exceptions to the grant of power...it might follow, by implication, that those rights that were not placed in that enumeration...were intended to be assigned into the hands of the General Government, and were consequently insecure."[5] Hardly the stuff of a big-government guy.

Hamilton also pleaded against "declaring that things shall not be done which there is no power to do," fearing the nation might one day look to the Bill of Rights to define our liberties and not to the body of the Constitution to define the government's power.[6] The framers' idea was to protect our natural rights by limiting the federal government, including the courts. If federal judges are the sole guardians of liberty, they not only have the power to uphold it, but also to take it away. The Constitution was to define our rights negatively by listing the few powers of government.

If we allow the federal judiciary to define our rights as expressed in the Bill of Rights, then they become whatever federal judges deem they ought to be. Inevitably, the federal bench either diminishes our freedoms or expands them beyond recognition. And when the court decides to apply the Bill of Rights to state law, it winds up trampling (as you will discover) on the most important safeguard of our liberties: the division of power between the federal and state governments. That is exactly what has happened through the legal phenomenon known as "incorporation doctrine."

Its dubious justification, which started in the early twentieth century, putatively resides within the Fourteenth Amendment's prohibitions against state law. Consequently, nearly every state legislature has now been forced to submit its every action to a review by the federal courts. As one of three Civil War Amendments, the Fourteenth was ratified in 1868, and declared, in its most potent clause, the following:

> No state shall make or enforce any law which shall abridge the privileges or immunities of citizens of the United States nor shall any state deprive any person of life, liberty, or property, without due process of law; nor deny to any person within its jurisdiction the equal protection of the laws. [7]

Ratified after the South's defeat, the Civil War Amendments were designed to constitutionalize the end of slavery in America. That laudable goal has regrettably grown to include the policy preferences of individual judges that have little to do with the plain language of a particular amendment.

In *Plyler v. Doe*, for example, a five-four majority distorted the meaning of "any person within its jurisdiction" in the Fourteenth Amendment to arrive at the conclusion that the state of Texas must provide a free public education to illegal immigrants.[8] But how can illegal aliens ever be subject to the jurisdiction of Texan authorities? It may or may not be smart public policy to provide such schooling, but it is not the Court's job to set social policy.

"Equal protection of the law" within the Amendment was an addendum whose intention was primarily aimed at eliminating the Black Codes that sprang up as a result of the South's defeat (but they were also prevalent in the North). In short, its original intent was to grant the rights of property, contract, and all the other liberties that were applicable to freemen at the time, to newly freed slaves. Surely a worthy goal and fairly easy to grasp. The law, whatever it is, should be applied in similar fashion to black and white. Unfortunately, it has been rendered into a blunt instrument, resulting in a myriad of court decisions shredding the concept to ribbons.[9]

Law professor Lino Graglia laments its modern incarnation having little to do with race when he notes that: "Not even a military school, the Court held in an opinion by Justice Ruth Bader Ginsberg, may operate as an all-male institution consistently with the Fourteenth Amendment."[10]

In *Grutter v. Bollinger*, the high court upheld an admissions plan at the University of Michigan law school that in point of fact denied equal access to the university based on race. The muddled thinking on the whole issue has gone from rejecting state discrimination to endorsing it. The high court seemed to frown upon explicit minority set asides in *Bakke* only to affirm a form of racial preference in *Grutter*—but only if it is narrowly tailored.[11] Finally, in a Washington school district case, the Court acknowledged Chief Justice John Robert's simple dictum, "The way to stop discrimination on the basis of race is to stop discriminating on the basis of race."[12] The result has been a hodgepodge of case law, leaving government subdivisions in the dark.

The Supreme Court did strike a bit of a blow for clarity in *Ricci*, the New Haven firefighter case at the heart of Justice Sonia Sotomayor's confirmation. The city of New Haven had refused to promote white employees based on an objective examination because they did better than black applicants. An appellate court ruling, joined by then Judge Sotomayor, sided with the city due to what it referred to as the "disparate impact" of employment evaluations.[13] The high court wisely ruled otherwise in a five-four decision, saying the city had violated Title VII of the 1964 Civil Rights Act and possibly equal protection under the Fourteenth Amendment.[14] In doing so it seemed to strike down quotas as a constitutional remedy for past discrimination and as a method to achieve racial balance. As two wrongs don't make a right, neither does reverse discrimination.

Unfortunately, "disparate impact" analysis is not going away, thanks to a 1971 Court decision that was effectively codified by the Civil Rights Act of 1991.[15] This is especially true in private employment discrimination cases, but state law has also been struck down due to a perceived bias. The result is a perpetual state of legal dysfunction, as nearly every law passed is bound to have a disproportionate effect on certain populations. In January 2010, a federal appeals court in Washington overturned a state law denying imprisoned felons the right to vote on the basis of its "disparate impact" on minorities disproportionately represented in correctional institutions.[16] The 2-1 ruling by a panel from the controversial 9th U.S. Circuit Court of Appeals overturned a district court ruling on the basis that the law was a violation of the Voting Rights Act of 1965. (The VRA of 1965 has also been used in this manner to draw electoral boundaries in order to property reflect minority representation. Critics assail such "gerrymandered" of Congressional districts as voting "quotas" designed to protect incumbents, and the high court has ruled on the legality of a number of statewide redistricting plans in recent years.)

But the law in this case was entirely equitable in that it denied elective franchise to white prisoners as well; apparently, it makes no difference under this bizarre legal analysis.

No such "disparate impact" silliness is needed for clear-cut cases of discrimination. Say what you will about the Supreme Court's decision in *Brown v. Board of Education of Topeka*; there was no doubt that forced segregation in schools was a classification based on race.[17] But even here the Court could not leave well enough alone. In 1971's *Swann v. Charlotte-Mecklenburg Schools* the justices decided that, contrary to the plain language of the Civil Rights Act of 1964, desegregation meant forced integration.[18]

Indeed, when the modern Court wants to legislate, they're unlikely to let much in the way of constitutional history stop them. On the same day justices ruled in *Brown*, they also addressed segregation in the District of Columbia. But since the Fourteenth Amendment's equal protection clause does not apply to federal territory, the justices simply relied upon "the "due process" clause of the Fifth Amendment, which does apply to the federal government."[19] The problem, as *Graglia* notes, is that the Fifth Amendment, unlike the Fourteenth, was "adopted in 1791 as part of a Constitution recognizing and protecting slavery."[20]

The document would have to be amended to end the shameful institution. But there could be no doubt that "due process" in the Fifth Amendment did not intend to end segregation when it was upholding slavery. The Court ignored the history and merely read into the clause what it desired—which it had been doing for some time.

By the middle of the twentieth century the "due process" clause within the Fourteenth Amendment had come to be seen as the catchall phrase for federal intervention—an intrusion that was not only unwarranted, but unnecessary.[21] To be sure, there are clear prohibitions against depriving one of life, liberty, or property without the due process of law in both the Fifth and Fourteenth Amendments. Those restrictions, however, were primarily aimed at protecting the accused in civil or criminal proceedings. Assuring a fair trial by one's peers, as well as many other generally accepted legal principles of traditional English common law, may all be considered part of "due process." But the phrase has little to say about the law itself. The modern court's so-called "substantive liberty interest" within the clause did.

Around the turn of the century the courts started to aggressively use the "due process" clause to somehow "apply the Bill of Rights to the states," thus "incorporating" federal judicial review over state legislation, as opposed to just legal procedures. As activist Lawrence Tribe admits, "Within a quarter century of the Fourteenth Amendment's adoption in 1868, the Supreme Court began striking down state laws on the basis of that amendment's "due process" clause because of particular substantive rights those laws infringed. By 1937 the Court had invalidated almost two hundred state laws on this ground." [22] Federal courts have since exploited this newfound power to strike down state and local laws governing term limits, welfare restrictions, religious displays, school prayer, prison reform, abortion rules, and the death penalty—almost anything you can imagine. [23]

Tribe, the influential professor from Harvard extols the modern view: "It is the guarantee of 'liberty' contained in the 'due process' clause, sometimes also called the liberty clause, of the Fourteenth Amendment that provides protection of our rights from infringement by the state governments. And the word 'liberty' simply is not self-defining." [24] This certainly seems at odds with the framers. Hamilton, on the eve of the

Constitutional Convention, described the legal history of the "due process" clause as having "a precise technical import... only applicable to the process and proceedings of courts of justice; they can never be referred to acts of the legislature."[25]

Chief Justice John Marshall concurred in 1833 when he explained in *Barron v. Baltimore* that the first eight amendments were clearly not intended for state law.[26] Recall, if you will, that the First Amendment begins with the words, "Congress shall make no law..." Jefferson would go so far as to claim, "While we deny that Congress has a right to control the freedom of the press, we have ever asserted the right of the states, and their exclusive right to do so."[27]

Jefferson was in fact an ardent advocate of free speech, but felt compelled to counter the prospect of federal intervention upon the states. To be sure, the idea of restricting any speech seems archaic, as it should, but its real-world application has not been so clear cut.

In *Tinker v. Des Moines Independent Community School District*, for example, the Supreme Court famously ruled that high school students do not "shed their constitutional rights to freedom of speech or expression at the schoolhouse door."[28] The lofty rhetoric sounds nice, but in the eyes of many administrators, the ability to discipline students for disruptive behavior has been seriously diminished. Indeed, the dissenting opinion in the case forewarned of such an outcome, suggesting, "if the time has come when pupils of state-supported schools...can defy and flout orders of school officials to keep their minds on their schoolwork, it is the beginning of a new revolutionary era of permissiveness in this country fostered by the judiciary."[29]

Federal enforcement of "First Amendment rights" has also been at the center of legal challenges (and victories) to local ordinances that reasonably restricted everything from child pornography to nude dancing—all the while making little distinction between "speech" and behavior.[30] Remarkably, the lawsuits themselves have been upheld on the flimsy basis of litigation as political speech.[31]

Applying the Bill of Rights to state law has unleashed an era of judicial activism, representing a great departure from our founding principles. In 1952, iconic Supreme Court Justice Robert Jackson took the revisionists head on when he said, "The history of criminal libel in America convinces me that the Fourteenth Amendment did not 'incorporate' the First...and because Congress probably could not enact this law it does not follow that the states may not."[32] The insistence by legal activists in overturning state law not only reveals little faith in our legal heritage but also shows a lack of confidence in the people's desire to protect their most cherished liberties. The fact is: a number of states have broader protections than that which the federal government might provide. [33]

"Incorporation doctrine" has also given us the rather whimsical notion that some rights are more equal than others. Liberal activists, for instance, disapprove of judicial scrutiny as it pertains to economic regulations. Again, this was not always so. During the *Lochner* era, the Supreme Court invalidated state interference in contract law, upholding the freedom to make voluntary economic arrangements. [34] This is an activist view of the Fourteenth Amendment, but at least consistent by including the obvious rights to property in a "substantive liberty interest."

Alas, the modern court invoked a grotesque double standard in *Gitlow v. New York* when it found only a select group of rights, such as freedom of the press, "among the fundamental personal rights and liberties protected by the "due process" clause of the Fourteenth Amendment from impairment by the states." [35] The 1925 decision became a watershed for the modern notion of "selective incorporation."

Even incorporating what the Court considers "fundamental" rights presents logical difficulties. In the late nineteenth century, the high court suggested that the procedural protections of due process in the Fourteenth Amendment were, in a general sense, a Fifth Amendment for the states.[36] Scholar Raoul Berger poses the obvious question: why would Congress consider free speech as part of "due process" in the Fifth Amendment when they had already guaranteed it in the First Amendment?[37] And if due process in the Fifth Amendment failed to define any "new" rights, the same language in the Fourteenth hardly could. Berger and others correctly assert that legitimate restrictions on the federal government were assigned by limiting its enumerated powers within the body of the Constitution, not by reading things into the Bill of Rights.

That is, unless you believe that the authors of the Fourteenth Amendment never had the Fifth in mind and actually meant to overturn the entire constitutional framework via the "due process" clause. Berger found little support for such a notion, finding that "Judge William Lawrence, a member of the thirty-ninth Congress, had quoted the Hamilton procedural definition in 1871; and in the same year another framer, James Garfield, said the due process of law meant 'an impartial trial according to the law of the land.'"[38] Noted Stanford Law School dean, John Hart Ely, also "found no references in the legislative history that gave the due process clause of the Fourteenth Amendment 'more than a procedural connotation...'"[39]

For some time, this notion of a procedural, and not "substantive," definition of "due process" held sway. In 1908, the Court wrote that "it is possible that some of the personal rights safeguarded by the first eight amendments against national action may also be safeguarded against state action," not because "those rights are enumerated in the first eight amendments, but because they are of such a nature that they are included in the conception of due process of law."[40] Justice Jackson later added, "The Fourteenth Amendment forbade states to deny the citizen due process of law. But it gave no notice to the people that its adoption would strip their local governments of power..."[41]

As recently as 1959, Supreme Court Justice Felix Frankfurter concurred, saying, "The relevant historical materials demonstrate conclusively that Congress, and the members of the legislatures of the ratifying states, did not contemplate that the Fourteenth Amendment was a shorthand incorporation of the first eight amendments making them applicable as explicit restrictions upon the states."[42]

Of course, there is room for legitimate debate even within a more traditional view of due process. The Supreme Court, for instance, has refused to overturn its landmark *Miranda* decision on the basis of established law and procedural safeguards in judicial hearings. The legal requirement of reading a suspect his or her rights was meant to prevent local authorities from conducting an interrogation so harsh that it "shocks the conscience" of the community.[43] Folks can debate what that means, but it still amounts to a procedural safeguard.

"There is simply no avoiding the fact," as Robert Bork would say, "that the word that follows 'due' is 'process.'"[44]

Regardless, the transformation seems complete and what was once a constitutional provision requiring procedural justice has been converted into a mechanism for federal judges to endlessly rule over laws whose substance they dislike. The judiciary has assumed the role of super legislature, and no state law is safe from the federal bench. In California, serial killer Richard Ramirez, sentenced to death in 1989 for the brutal rape and murder of at least thirteen people, still sits on death row due to an appeals process that likely won't end before his natural death in prison.[45] This is dysfunctional government.

Perhaps the most controversial and well-known decision in judicial overreach involved the beginning of life, not the end. Prior to *Roe v. Wade*, a mother and a father who disagree on the fate of their unborn child would argue the case in state court. The decision in *Roe* found, as described in dissent, "a new constitutional right for pregnant mothers," while the majority cited "the concept of liberty guaranteed by the first section of the Fourteenth Amendment" to strike down state antiabortion statutes.[46] Subsequent cases have refined the issue but, as late as 1992 in *Casey,* the Supreme Court found state laws requiring a woman to notify her husband before having an abortion to be an "undue burden" on "privacy."[47] Originalists correctly assert that since the Constitution is silent on the issue of abortion (as it is with the death penalty and most matters of criminal law); the federal government has neither the power to protect nor proscribe it. *Roe*, by judicial fiat, ruled otherwise.

The ruling was so divisive precisely because it expanded upon a litany of unprecedented "privacy" rights nowhere to be found in our nation's legal heritage. Before the modern era, most scholars would have been hardpressed to cite an instance of, say, federal law being struck down by the "due process" clause in the Fifth Amendment, let alone on the basis of a so-called "privacy right."

"The fact that a majority of the states," wrote associate justice William Rehnquist, "had restrictions on abortions for at least a century is a strong indication, it seems to me, that the asserted right to an abortion is not so rooted in the traditions and conscience of our people as to be ranked as fundamental."[48] Indeed, there were thirty-six states with laws limiting abortion when the Fourteenth Amendment was adopted, and most of them stayed on the books for the next century.

Roe's "exercise of raw judicial power" was even blasted by a few pro-choice advocates who said that reading abortion rights in the "due process" clause was "not constitutional law and gives almost no sense of an obligation to try to be."[49]

Unfortunately, judicial activism can be contagious. A few social conservatives now assert that the "due process" clause of the Fourteenth Amendment can be used to force states to rewrite their criminal codes to ban abortion throughout the states.[50] Yet the original intention of the "due process" clause, as we have seen, was "simply a requirement that the substance of any law be applied to a person through fair procedures by any tribunal hearing a case. The clause says nothing whatever about what the substance of the law must be."[51]

No matter one's view on the issue, exploiting the "due process" clause for the "pro-life" side of the issue is no less a misreading of the Constitution than the judicial nonsense mandating "abortion rights." While some states have expanded some so-called privacy protections, they are under no federal requirement to do so. In fact, genuine rights to privacy have been clearly expressed in the Constitution or in longstanding common law. A prudent person might find a "reasonable expectation of privacy" in a number of circumstances, but it remains more than a little difficult to see how a right to abortion is among them.[52]

The judicial alchemy seems to have caught up with the Court, as it now routinely gives what appears to be conflicting views on the issue of privacy and local law. In 2005 the justices gave the federal government the power to regulate medicinal marijuana; a year later it ruled to let the states decide on physician-assisted suicide.[53] Apparently, the fundamental "right to be let alone" is proving difficult in practice.[54] Is there a right to privacy, for example, in a hotel room? Sure you say, but what if the proprietor reserves a contractual right to check on the room for possible violations of a no-smoking policy? The ACLU has even claimed that individuals who have sex in public restrooms have a "reasonable expectation of privacy."[55]

Overturning state law based on the flimsiest notions of "privacy" is fraught with problems. Most crimes after all are committed "in private"; of course there can be no right to privacy if it infringes on another. If the plain meaning of the Constitution gives way to an activist court's newfound "privacy" rights, then how it is that any consensual activity isn't a constitutional right? Yet states throughout American history have consistently reserved the right (for better or worse) to declare a number of arrangements between consenting adults illegal, from prostitution to illicit drug use to usury.

In fact, usurping the sovereign power of state legislatures has left the nation polarized in such a manner not seen since the aftermath of the Dred Scott decision—which ironically also cited "due process" in its opinion.[56] This has also turned the courts into three-ring political circuses. If Americans on the left and right truly wish to live and let live, then return the most troubling social issues to the states, and let the people once again choose the laws under which they live, provided they are applied equally.

Libertarians fear such an outcome, presumably based on fears of a local nanny state. Law professor Richard Epstein, for instance, asserts that the states' police power must be constrained by the legal precedents of tort law, or else our freedoms would be subject to the whim of local officials.[57] For the record, I happen to agree with the critics on the futility of most "crimes" between two consenting adults; enforcement seldom works (see prohibition and the war on drugs) and ends up creating more problems than it solves. There is a difference, as they say, between a crime and a sin.

But herein lies the rub: just who decides when a third party is harmed? The knee-jerk response is, "The courts!" The next chapter looks into why that is not always the best answer. But for now, consider this: pro-life judges have just as much medical knowledge as pro-choice ones, yet both sides disagree on the status of a fetus. Deferring questions of social policy to a wide range of people through their elected representatives remains the best solution.

The Fourteenth Amendment was not meant as a "perpetual censor upon all legislation of the states," as the majority in the 1873 *Slaughter-House* cases declared.[58] *Slaughter-House* has been much maligned by well-intentioned critics, such as Epstein, et al. They cite dissenting Justice Stephen Field, who said in a subsequent case, "No one has ever pretended... that the Fourteenth Amendment interferes in any respect with the police power of the state," nevertheless the state should "not be permitted to encroach upon any of the just rights of the citizen, which the Constitution intended to guard against abridgment."[59] The Court still seems to be discovering those "just" rights.

The majority of justices in *Slaughter-House*, far closer in time to the original intent of the Fourteenth Amendment, ruled that it did not preclude the states from passing regulations (granted, most in the economic arena remain counterproductive). Four years later the high court seemed to reaffirm its position, suggesting that contrary to the critics, the *Slaughter-House* cases were no aberration. In *Munn v.*

Illinois, the court was succinct, "For protection against abuse by legislatures, the people must resort to the polls, not the courts."[60]

The core problem for those who seek such an expansive view of federally enforced "rights" is that they've yet to offer an adequate mechanism—other than increasingly unreliable courts—for the resolution of competing interests when these "just rights" collide. That's why regardless of one's particular view of abortion, or any other social controversy, most matters of intrastate criminal law reside with the states and the common law. The Constitution was written to defend the nation while simultaneously protecting the states and the people from the new central government. The states were to keep the power to protect residents from one another pursuant to their own state charters.

CHAPTER 3 NOTES

1. *Hale v. Hinkel*, 201 U.S. 43, 50 LEd. 652, 20 S.Ct. 370, Supreme Court of the United States, 1906.

2. See Alexander Hamilton, James Madison, and John Jay, *The Federalist Papers*, edited by Michael L. Chadwick, (Washington: Global Affairs Publishing Co., 1987)

3. Benno Schmidt, Joseph Ellis, and Sean Wilentz, C-SPAN, "James Madison and the Constitution," New York Historical Society Panel Discussion, October 2, 2008. http://www.c-spanvideo.org/program/281562-1.(Accessed March 2010). Madison sponsored the Bill of Rights in 1789, using the works of such strong anti-federalists as George Mason.

4. Banning, *The Sacred Fire,* 117, 118.

5. Robert H. Bork, *The Tempting of America* (New York: The Free Press, 1990) 185. It's also one reason he insisted on the Ninth Amendment, reserving "other rights retained by the people."

6. Hamilton, "Federalist 84," *The Federalist Papers*, 465.

7. Robert L. Lineberry, George C. Edwards, and Martin P. Wattenberg, *Government in America* (New York: Harper Collins Publishers, 1991) 125. Section 2 of the Fourteenth Amendment also tried to ensure voting rights for newly freed slaves and gave Congress power to enforce through legislation.

8. See *Plyler v. Doe, 457 U.S. 202 (1982)*.

9.   Lineberry, et al, *Government in America*. Indeed, the level of judicial review over state law is dependent upon the legislation. Race-based classifications are *inherently suspect*, demanding *strict scrutiny* of a *compelling state interest* to satisfy equal protection. Others must merely be *substantially related* to a *legitimate state interest*, while yet others must bear only a *rational relationship* or be deemed *reasonable*.

10. Lino A. Graglia, *Constitutional Law without the Constitution: The Supreme Court's Remaking of America*, Robert H. Bork ed., (Stanford, CA: Hoover Institution Press, 2005) 31. Separate but equal was traditionally a defense in gender classifications by the state for personal privacy reasons.

11. Robert A. Levy and William Mellor, *The Dirty Dozen* (Sentinel Publishing, 2008) 204. Justice O'Connor majority opinion in *Grutter,* noting "a compelling state interest in student body diversity" as well as the supposed "educational benefits" that flow from it caused the Court to allow the Michigan law school to deny access to a white student though her admission test scores were higher than minority applicants.

12. The quote was part of Roberts' opinion in the Seattle case where a school district's policy to assign students for the purposes of racial integration was overturned, though the Court's plurality opinion said the case was not governed by *Grutter*. *Parents Involved in Community Schools v. Seattle School District No. 1, 551 U.S. 701 (2007).*

13. *Griggs v. Duke Power Co.*, 401 U.S. 424 (1971). In *Griggs*, the Supreme Court declared that "even where an employer is not motivated by discriminatory intent," employers are nonetheless prohibited from "using a facially neutral employment practice that has an unjustified adverse impact on members of a protected class."

14. See *Ricci v Destafano (2009).*

15. *Alexander v. Sandoval, 532 U.S. 275 (2001)*. Though the convoluted analysis that came out of *Griggs* is usually reserved for private acts of discrimination pursuant to "civil rights law" under Congress' authority to regulate interstate commerce, the rationale has been increasingly used to strike down state regulation, notwithstanding the ruling in *Ricci*. In the 2001 case of *Alexander v. Sandoval*, the Court however reiterated that Congress had not intended to give disparate impact such weight with regard to state regulations.

16. Rachel LaCorte, *Associated Press*, 5 January 2010.

17. Bork, *The Tempting of America*, 82. Some originalists disagree on whether *Brown* can be justified by the Fourteenth Amendment given that the civil rights laws at the time seemed to sanction separate but equal. Bork however comes down squarely in favor of the initial holding in *Brown*, suggesting that the ratifiers of the Fourteenth Amendment were not explicitly addressing segregation and that "it had been apparent for some time that segregation rarely if ever produced equality," thus the Court could either "abandon the quest for equality by allowing segregation or to forbid segregation in order to achieve equality. There was no third choice. Either choice would violate one aspect of the original understanding..."

18. Graglia, *Constitutional Law*, 45.

19. Ibid., 23.

20. Ibid.

21. *People v. Goodwin*, 18 R. Johns, 187 N.Y. 1820. Though Chief Justice Spencer of New York believed that the Fifth Amendment prohibition of double jeopardy applied to state tribunals, he nonetheless reiterated its existence long before the Bill of Rights, "I do not consider it material whether this provision be considered as extending to the state tribunals or not; the principle is a sound and fundamental one, that no man shall be twice put in jeopardy of life or limb for the same offense." The opinion invoked "some of the plainest and best established principles in relation to the rights of the citizens, and the rules of common law."

22. Lawrence Tribe, *Abortion: The Clash of Absolutes*, (New York: W.W. Norton, 1990) 84.

23. Orrin G. Hatch, "A Circuitous Court," *The Washington Times*, 2 July 2002. The somewhat infamous Ninth Circuit Court of Appeals in California has engaged in a particularly blatant exercise of judicial legislation, striking down "under God" in the Pledge of Allegiance as unconstitutional and declaring the right to bear arms does not apply to individuals, though the Supreme Court has since found otherwise. Not surprisingly, the Ninth happens to be the most overturned appeals court in the land.

24. Tribe, *Abortion*, 83. Interestingly enough, Tribe goes on to admit, "The application of the Bill of Rights to the states, although not specifically intended by the framers of the Fourteenth Amendment and although once highly controversial, is now common ground." Ibid., 87.

25. Raoul Berger, *The Fourteenth Amendment and the Bill of Rights*, (Norman: University of Oklahoma, 1989) 9.

26. Smith, *The Constitution*, 101.

27. Berger, *The Fourteenth Amendment*, 13. Jefferson's letter to Abigail Adams, September 11, 1804.

28. Richard Arum, *Judging School Discipline* (Cambridge: Harvard University Press, 2003) 61.

29. Ibid.

30. Graglia, *Constitutional Law*, 29.

31. Ibid.

32. Jackson's dissent in *Beauharnais v Illinois*, 343 U.S. 250 (1952).

33. Ellen Paul, "Taking Liberty," *Reason*, March 1984, 49. Several states modified their takings provisions in the 1870s to allow compensation for "damaged" property. The Constitution of the State of Minnesota for example arguably provides enhanced protection for property owners with regard to state condemnation in Article 1, Section 13: Private property shall not be taken, destroyed or damaged for public use without just compensation therefore, first paid or secured. Constitution of the State of Minnesota, Adopted October 13, 1857* Generally revised November 5, 1974. Further amended November 1974, 1980, 1982, 1984, 1988, 1990, 1996, 1998, 2006, and 2008.

34. *Lochner v. New York*, 198 U.S. (1905). Tribe quotes Oliver Wendell Holmes' famous dissent in the 1905 decision, "the Fourteenth Amendment does not enact Mr. Herbert Spencer's Social Statistics."

35. Lineberry, et al, *Government in America*, 125.

36. *Hurtado v. California*, 110 U.S. 516 (1884). The Court went so far as to intimate that due process in the Fourteenth Amendment did not even encompass everything in the Fifth, such as right to a grand jury, but instead "refers to that law of the land in each state which derives its authority from the inherent and reserved powers of the state..."

37. Berger, *The Fourteenth Amendment,* 12, 13.

38. Ibid., 10, 11.

39. Ibid.

40. Manion, *Cancer in the Constitution*, 23, 24. Quoting *Twining v. New York* (1908).

41. Jackson's somewhat famous dissent in *Terminiello v. Chicago*, 337 U.S. 1 (1949).

42. Berger, *The Fourteenth Amendment*, 8.This was directly counter to Justice Hugo Black's contention a decade earlier that the Bill of Rights, in his view, was incorporated.

43. See *Rochin v. California*, 342 U.S. (1952).

44. Bork, *The Tempting of America*, 32.

45. Ed Barnes, "In California, Killers Sit on 'Symbolic' Death Row for Decades, Costing Billions," *FOXNews*, 22 March 2010. (Accessed March 2010)

46. Rehnquist dissent in *Roe v Wade*, 410 U.S. 113 (1973).

47. *Planned Parenthood of Southeastern Pennsylvania v. Casey*, 505 U.S. 833 (1992).

48. Rehnquist dissent in *Roe v Wade*, 410 U.S. 113 (1973).

49. John Hart Ely, "*Roe v Wade* at 25: Still Illegitimate," *The Wall Street Journal*, 22 January 1998, A18. Quoting from dissent in *Roe v. Wade*, 410 U.S. 113 (1973).

50. "Ashcroft's Statement on Abortion," *Human Events*, 29 May 1998, 7.

51. Bork, *The Tempting of America*, 30, 31, 44.

52. *Katz v. United States*, 386 U.S. 954 (1967). The 1967 *Katz* decision in (overturning *Olmstead v. United States* in 1928), declared that actions deemed in violation of someone's "reasonable expectation of privacy" were no longer constitutional in the opinion of the Court. The Court had already extended Fourth Amendment rights against state action in *Mapp v. Ohio* and even Justice Antonin Scalia's majority opinion in *Kyllo v. U.S.* upheld the express prohibition against unreasonable searches and seizures, striking down a state's use of high-tech thermal imaging devices without probable cause. That however is a far cry from finding new implied rights to privacy.

53. See *Gonzales v. Oregon*, 546 U.S. 243 (2006) and *Gonzales v. Raich*, 545 U.S.1 (2005).

54. *Olmstead v. United States*, 277 U.S. 438 (1928). See Judge Louis Brandies famous dissent in a 1928 case upholding federal wiretapping.

55. www.startribune.com/local/13817377.html?pt=y (Accessed April 2010)

56. McDonald, *States' Rights*, 179; Harry V. Jaffa, *A New Birth of Freedom*, (Lanham: Roman & Littlefield Publishers, Inc., 2000) 175. Chief Justice Roger Taney cited the Fifth Amendment's due process clause to deny the right of free states to ban slavery for newly arrived citizens. Effectively overturning the Missouri Compromise, Taney stated, "An act of Congress which deprives a citizen of the United States of his liberty or property... could hardly be dignified with the name of due process of law." The court in *Dred Scott* was in fact ruling on federal legislation before the passage of the Civil War Amendments and many had already thought that the Kansas-Nebraska Act's endorsement of "popular sovereignty," as espoused by legislative author Sen. Stephen Douglas, simply codified state control on the issue of slavery, one way or another. Scholar Harry Jaffa writes, however, that the decision in *Scott* went much further, holding there "was no power under the Constitution, either in Congress or in a territorial legislation, to exclude slavery from a territory...Taney's dicta became "rights" that were inviolable by majorities. But as Lincoln repeatedly pointed out, these same dicta contained premises that could logically lead to the further conclusion that there was no power under the Constitution for any *state* to exclude slavery."

57. Richard Epstein, *How Progressives Rewrote the Constitution*, (Cato Institute, 2006) 45. "In principle, there is no doubt that the police power should cover those cases in which an individual, acting alone or in combination with others, causes harm to a third person, where *harm* tracks the meaning it has in the tort law—damage to persons, chattels, or reputation."

58. *Slaughter-House Cases 83 U.S. 36 (1873)*.

59. *Bartemeyer v. Iowa, 85 U.S. 18 Wall. 129 129 (1873)*.

60. *Munn v. Illinois, 94 U.S. 113 (1877)*.

CHAPTER 4

Don't Trust the Courts

THE MODERN INTERPRETATION of so-called "privacy rights" began with the case of *Griswold v. Connecticut* in 1965. Justice William O. Douglas cited a "marital privacy" within the "penumbras" and "emanations" of rights implied in the Constitution to strike down a Connecticut law prohibiting the use of contraceptives.[1] As Justice Potter Stewart said in dissent, it makes no difference that the law may have been "uncommonly silly," there was simply "no such general right of privacy" in the Fourteenth Amendment.[2] Justice Black, also weighed in, chiding that "The Court talks about a constitutional 'right of privacy' as though there is some constitutional provision or provisions forbidding any law ever to be passed which might abridge the 'privacy' of individuals. But there is not."[3]

Griswold was decided 7-2 with a concurring opinion citing the Ninth Amendment by Justice Arthur Goldberg. Though two others signed on to Goldberg's opinion, Douglas himself saw a problem expanding the Ninth Amendment, later admitting in *Roe* that "The Ninth Amendment obviously does not create federally enforceable rights."[4] Regardless, the genie was out of the bottle, and the Ninth has proved to be one of the new gateways to a whole host of fictitious rights, including the right to taxpayer-funded healthcare.[5]

In what appears to be stunning new scholarship, however, Loyola Law Professor Kurt Lash contends that the bulk of Ninth Amendment jurisprudence is simply wrong. Far from interpreting the Amendment's guarantee of "other rights retained by the people" as empowering the courts, Lash reveals its actual meaning as a reinforcement of federalism.[6] Put together with the Tenth Amendment, writes Lash, "The historical Ninth Amendment strongly suggests that the Constitution was to be construed in a manner that preserves as much as possible the people's right to local self-government."[7]

As we have noted, the Bill of Rights was itself insisted upon by those fearful of federal power. Yet, according to judicial activists, the Fourteenth Amendment incorporates federal power against the states. This is circular reasoning, turning constitutional history on its head. For example, abolitionists declined to cite the Ninth Amendment as a pretext to end slavery, an odd position to take, given that slavery violates just about every aspect of "privacy" one could imagine. On the other hand, those advocating the right of secession were much more inclined to do so.[8] In short, both the Ninth and Tenth Amendments were added to the Bill of Rights to bolster the power of the states.

Lash recounts the words of Louisiana senator Judah P. Benjamin on the floor of the Senate in 1860: "So, sir, we find that not alone in these two conventions, but by the common action of the states, there was an important addition made to the Constitution by which it was expressly provided that it should not be construed to be a General Government over all the people, but that it was a Government of States, which delegated powers to the General Government. The language of the ninth and tenth amendments to the Constitution is susceptible of no other construction: 'The enumeration in the Constitution of certain rights shall not be construed to deny or disparage others retained by the people.'"[9]

That is, the "textual mandate" is one of majoritarian rights "retained by the people" in the several states;[10] in other words, according to Lash, "the right to local self-government in all matters not delegated to the federal government."[11]

The federal judiciary has come under fire for more than just Ninth Amendment jurisprudence. During the 1960s, the high court became synonymous with all that was wrong with the federal bench—especially in the area of criminal justice. The Court's decisions alienated so many Americans, there was even a movement, albeit fractured, to impeach its chief justice, Earl Warren. Eschewing deference to the elected branches of government, the majority saw fit to strike down a whole host of laws enacted legislatively based on what they considered a more enlightened view of the Constitution.

And though a few decisions seemed to have a clever kernel of truth to them, the justices repeatedly stretched their interpretations to arrive at the public policy outcomes they so desperately desired. In 1963, Gideon interpreted a constitutional right to counsel to mean that taxpayers should foot the bill (as opposed to, say, the ACLU). *Escobedo* and *Miranda* held that voluntary criminal confessions would be inadmissible should the police question a suspect before the defendant's rights are read; and in 1972, with Warren's legacy firmly intact, the high court ruled that the death penalty, when applied with indiscretion (whatever that meant) was unconstitutional.[12]

Old habits die hard and, as recently as 2008, the Court continued its confusion over capital punishment when it refused to allow the execution of someone convicted of the violent rape of a child.[13]

This activism was a stark departure from not only America's legal heritage, but our social custom as well. By "incorporating" the establishment clause of the First Amendment, for instance, decades if not centuries of religious practice came under attack.[14] Starting with *Cantwell* in 1940, the "court held for the first time that the "due process" clause of the Fourteenth Amendment applies to states the First Amendment's guarantee of religious freedom..."[15]

A litany of cases followed, redefining American tradition by confusing freedom of religion with freedom from religion. There is a difference between religion as state policy (something to be avoided) and attempting to remove any aspect of religion from public life. But the numerous instances of faith officially reflected in American history haven't stopped the Court from removing nondenominational prayer and religious displays from schools as well as commencements.[16] Or from requiring that local governments jump through an elaborate set of hoops known as the "Lemon test" if they wished to avoid "establishing" a religion by erecting a Christmas display.[17]

Ironically, even the legitimate goals of "due process" have been abused by an activist bench. Our legal traditions rely on a venerable English system, which had very few statutes guiding it; judges in those days decided disputes based on not only equitable remedies but ancient social custom. The old common law would dissect different circumstances with a process that continually clarified the law, thereby setting a legal precedent that "can only be disturbed by private parties bringing new cases with slightly different circumstances or new arguments."[18] As the law is perfected, "fewer and fewer such cases will be brought...parties then bargain 'in the shadow of settled law,' dividing a larger pie than they would under rules not tested over time,"[19]

Because of this, once a ruling was made, it became the "law at common" and the "principle of adhering to precedent" was to be revered. That principle is also known as the doctrine of *stare decisis*, Latin for "to stand by that which is decided."[20] In no small matter, the doctrine of court precedent has safeguarded the traditional rights of due process, such as the presumption of innocence until guilt is proven beyond a reasonable doubt—or in civil matters, until a preponderance of the evidence demonstrates otherwise.[21] Even the right to a trial by a jury of peers, though noted in the Constitution, has long been custom because "the historical foundations for these principles extends down centuries into the common law."[22]

But the common law has done more than just safeguard due process—it has been the very bulwark of our liberties since the Magna Carta.[23] By viewing human relations through the prism of a higher law, the old law came up with two fundamental rules: "Do not encroach on other persons or their property and do all you have agreed to do."[24] Essentially, the law of torts and of contracts—the heart and soul of American jurisprudence. These natural laws are immutable and can never really—in the lexicon of legal activists—evolve.

In its purest form, the common law doctrine adhered to these principles and was in fact superior in many ways to a statutory scheme.[25] Juries, able to take case by case, and consider the extenuating circumstances of each episode, are better suited to impartial justice than bureaucrats or lawmakers who are subject to political interests eager to violate longstanding rules for their own benefit. Unfortunately, this restrained approach, utilizing narrow legal rulings, has given way to sweeping verdicts that routinely supplant the virtue of precedent. In short, the modern courts have entered the realm of policy-making.

A fine example is the now somewhat infamous McDonald's coffee verdict in 1994. The jury in the case awarded the plaintiff $2.7 million (reduced to a mere $640,000 on appeal) ostensibly to send a message about hot coffee at the fast food chain.[26] Yet, if the public felt that the merchant was serving a dangerous product (depending upon what the meaning of the word "hot" is), then the political constituents, and not one runaway jury, ought to legislate a ban on such commerce. The old common law would have looked at this as a contract: someone pays for hot coffee and they get hot coffee; case closed. The memorable McDonald's coffee verdict is just another form of judicial activism.

When courts abandon the principles of contract, there ceases to be the certainty of agreed upon rules. Is 180-degree coffee too hot? What about 175 degrees? Our liberties are often safeguarded best by the elected branches of government. It is true, special interests are always present in any political decision, but they have infiltrated the courtroom as well.

And when the courts go astray, the political system actually becomes more predictable as every party to a controversy gets a say in the electoral process. More important, as federal judge Alex Kozinski observed, "It is a strength of our federal system that states can serve as laboratories for experimenting with various legislative judgments"—even over coffee.[27]

Perhaps the best example, however, of recent judicial policy-making was the bizarre litigation over tobacco. Billions of dollars have changed hands (most of it going into the pockets of trial lawyers and into the hands of politicians) in monetary settlements based on little more than legal extortion. Third parties, stepping into the shoes of smokers (a legal doctrine known as subrogation) traditionally would be subject to any customary defense that the tobacco industry could assert, including assumption of risk.[28] But when state governments and insurance companies sought and won billions for health-related expenses as a result of their own fiscal decisions, they did so in large part by stripping away these legal defenses.

If I buy a brand-new sports car and it doesn't run or is defective in some other way, it's a violation of contract. If the defect causes an accident, it will probably be both an infringement on contract and a tort, allowing me to recover not only the purchase price but damages for an injury. Yet not all damages are equal. If I buy the car and decide to go racing, then I have assumed the risk of injury. Likewise, mountain-climbing is inherently dangerous; if the law allowed climbers to sue their guide for every loose rock that causes a fall, no matter how trivial, you can imagine the legal chaos.

That's why few things are more crucial to the law than that of consent. As MIT engineer, Harvard lawyer, and author Peter Huber put it, the "old common law took the concept seriously enough to render it in Latin," *volenti non fit injuria* (to one who is willing, no wrong is done).[29] To disregard it is to disregard the law of contracts, one of the pillars of American jurisprudence. If in fact states were really concerned over the health-related expenses of smoking, forthright solutions were always evident for anyone to see. If legislators really wanted to stop paying for smoking-related illnesses, then stop. Or better yet, just ban tobacco use entirely. If tobacco executives were engaged in a deliberate conspiracy to "kill people" (to use the plaintiff lawyers' hyperbole), then criminally charge them.

The tobacco lawsuits occurred not because of public demand. Far from it, outright prohibition would never pass most legislative bodies. No, the litigation lottery was driven solely by money and politics. Money for the lawyers and a stepping stone for ambitious attorneys general, the only casualty was the law.

Besides, there was very little evidence when taxes and fees were considered (which they were not) that smokers cost governments anything; the reverse is more likely. Governments had "unclean hands" by licensing tobacco and reaping the tax windfall from cigarettes for decades. Our common law heritage used to require actual damages before most legal actions could be sustained. The undoing of those precious legal defenses, such as subrogation, assumption of risk, and traditional rules of causation have now allowed similarly weak cases to move forward against other parties, such as obesity claims against fast food chains.

Perhaps a legal backlash of sorts is brewing. Subsequent lawsuits filed by insurance companies and union health funds, hoping to cash in on the earlier Medicaid-reimbursement bonanza, have been met with stinging rebukes. Just after some of the tobacco verdicts, the Seventh Circuit Court of Appeals appeared to invoke a bit of consumer responsibility, at least when it comes to notions of holding all business strictly liable. "The food industry," it said, "puts refined sugar in many products, making them more tasty; as a result some people eat too much (or eat the wrong things) and suffer health problems and early death. No one supposes, however, that sweet foods are defective products on this account; chocoholics can't recover in tort from Godiva Chocolatier. If, as the Funds and Blues say, the difference is that Phillip Morris has committed civil wrongs while Godiva has not, then the way to establish this is though tort suits, rather than through litigation in which the plaintiffs seek to strip their adversaries of all defenses." [30]

Indeed, the recent explosion of punitive damage awards (those above and beyond compensatory relief) combined with the perverse incentives of contingency fees have resulted in a number of products being litigated nearly out of existence—from breast implants to small aircraft. Notwithstanding a few sensible court rulings to the contrary (See *BMW v. Gore; Exxon;* and *State Farm)* in which the Court said that excessive punitive damage awards based on a defendant's wealth, or deep pockets was entering "the zone of arbitrariness that violates the Due Process Clause," lower courts continue to allow what many see as excessive judgments.[31] "In 1999 alone, the top ten verdicts totaled nine billion dollars, triple the amount for 1998 and twelve times the amount for 1997."[32] These excessive awards, even if reduced on appeal, are justified by the trial bar as a means to punish wayward corporations—but isn't that what a criminal justice system is for?[33]

The courts are there to settle disputes according to the law. But too many judges have moved away from their traditional role as referee of agreed-upon rules and on to the crafting of what they think those rules should be. "What you are talking about today, sir, is war...we are going to see things we have never seen in the history of American tort law," so says Victor E. Schwartz, a former plaintiff attorney and co-author of *Cases and Materials on Torts*.[34] The delicate balance of power has already been substantially altered by granting the judiciary unenumerated power to decide those matters best left to the political branches of government.

It becomes especially dangerous when we consolidate judicial power at the federal level. When the Supreme Court justices get it wrong, there simply is no final appeal. And wrong they have been.

The high court has systematically excluded protections for economic freedoms while raising judicial scrutiny for others. Not long after the turn of the twentieth century, the court carved out its policy of "selective incorporation" in *Gitlow* by protecting only those rights it deemed "fundamental."[35] Yet it's hard to imagine what could be more personal than the right to property. Pennsylvania delegate to the Constitutional Convention, Gouverneur Morris, said the preservation of property was the "principal object of government," echoing a Lockean liberalism. He even went so far as to consider excluding elective franchise to those without property. "Give the votes to people who have no property and they will sell them to the rich who will be able to buy them." [36] At least *Lochner* and its libertarian supporters had consistency on their side, coming down squarely in favor of liberty to contract.[37] In fact, the demise of contractual rights embedded in *Lochner* should serve as an embarrassing reminder of the Supreme Court's capriciousness when it gets to define which rights are worth upholding.

When it comes to property, more recent Court decisions are even less reassuring. In *Kelo v. City of New London* the justices upheld a Connecticut municipality's attempts to condemn private homes for an economic development project, which to date has failed to materialize.[38] The limited power of eminent domain was to be utilized in accordance with "just compensation" for the necessary execution of a "public use," say, an armory or perhaps a road.[39] Not for the benefit of a private interest.

Unfortunately, the power of condemnation is now routinely used on so-called "blighted" areas, the result of which has been the destruction of single-family homes and small businesses standing in the way of so-called redevelopment efforts. No doubt, previous rulings had laid the foundation for these "urban renewal" schemes.[40] But it was the *Kelo* decision that sparked national outrage and led to a myriad of state reforms restricting the power of eminent domain.[41]

Madison, who once declared as a "man is said to have a right to his property, he may be equally said to have a property in his rights," would have shuddered at such a cavalier attitude towards property.[42] That's one reason he insisted on protection against government "takings" in the first place.[43] For good reason, without the fundamental right to property as a barrier against the state, the Fourth Amendment's prohibition against unreasonable search and seizure, for example, has little meaning. As Justice Stewart once asserted, "the dichotomy between personal liberties and property rights is a false one. Property does not have rights. The rights to enjoy property without unlawful deprivation no less than the right to speak or the right to travel is in truth a 'personal' right...a fundamental interdependence exists between the personal right to liberty and the personal right to property. Neither could have meaning without the other."[44]

CHAPTER 4 NOTES

1. *Griswold v. Connecticut,* 38 U.S. 479 (1965).

2. Bork, *The Tempting of America*, 100.

3. Ibid.

4. Tim Cavanaugh, "Ninth Configurations," *Reason*, February 2010, 62, 63.

5. Ibid., Liberals routinely cite "vistas of positive rights," including the right to taxpayer-funded healthcare, as enforceable by the Ninth Amendment's rights "retained by the people."

6. Kurt T. Lash, *The Lost History of the Ninth Amendment* (New York: Oxford, 2009).

7. Ibid., xix.

8. Ibid., 240-41.

9. Ibid., 241-42.

10. Ibid., xix.

11. Ibid., 249.

12. Smith, *The Constitution,* 118, 119.

13. See *Kennedy v. Louisiana*, 544 U.S. __ (2008). In *Roper* two years earlier, the high court ruled that capital punishment for a crime committed as a juvenile was also unconstitutional.

14. "Congress shall make no law respecting the establishment of religion, or prohibiting the free exercise thereof..." reads the opening phrase of the First Amendment. U.S. Constitution, Philadelphia, 1787.

15. Smith, *The Constitution,* 109.

16. E. Christian Kopff, *The Devil Knows Latin*, (Wilmington: ISI Books 2001) 57, 58.

17. Ibid., In 1971's *Lemon v. Kurtzman,* the Court advanced a three-pronged test for a religious activity to survive "establishment" scrutiny. 1) It must have a secular purpose, 2) It must neither advance nor inhibit religion, and 3) it must not foster an entanglement with religion. Critics argue this is clear policy-making disguised as law.

18. Lynn Scarlett, *Reason*, May 1996, 23.

19. Ibid.

20. Steven Brill, (Editor), *The Court TV Cradle to Grave Legal Survival Guide*, (New York: American Lawyer/Little, Brown, and Co. 1995) 413.

21. It wasn't, however, until 1970, in *Winship* 397 U.S. 358 (1970) that the United States Supreme Court actually declared that the beyond a reasonable doubt standard in criminal law was a federal constitutional requirement in guilty verdicts—which suggests that when it comes to those procedural guarantees that constitute the difference between a trial and lynch mob, the old common law was ahead of the game.

22. *Apprendi v. New Jersey 530 U.S. 466 (200).*

23. *National Archives and Records Administration*, Washington D.C. In 1297, the Magna Carta was confirmed by Edward I and recorded as English statute. In the early seventeenth century, Sir Edward Coke raised it in opposition to the tyranny of the Stuart kings and it has since been used as a model for the enumeration rights throughout the West, including in the American Revolution and the Bill of Rights.

24. Richard J. Maybury, *Whatever Happened to Justice?* (Placerville: Bluestocking Press, 1993) 31.

25. Ibid., 128. Though ideally, good law should only be a "rewrite of case law...to summarize and clarify common law, not overturn it."

26. C. Boyden Gray, "Damage Control," *The Wall Street Journal*, 11 December 2002, A18. The McDonald's case is just one example our litigation explosion. According to former White House legal counsel, C. Boyden Gray, "the legal system's direct costs are more than $180 billion annually, roughly two percent of GDP. Furthermore, less than half of the money spent on tort litigation goes toward compensation."

27. Alex Kozinski, "The Case of Punitive Damages v. Democracy, *The Wall Street Journal*, 19 January 1995, A16.

28. Epstein, *How Progressives,* 45, 46. This was not the first time such favoritism has been shown to the plaintiff. Epstein notes that similar attempts were done at the state and federal level supposedly aimed at "protecting workers by limiting or striking down assumption of risk" in the early twentieth century. The tobacco case just happened to be the most brazen in its legal and financial outcome.

29. Peter Huber, *Liability: The Legal Revolution and Its Consequences* (New York: Basic Books, 1988) 20.

30. Review & Outlook, "Smoked Out," *The Wall Street Journal*, 13 December 1999, A14.

31. Dick Thornburgh, "No End in Sight as Punitive Damages Go Up, Up, Up," *The Wall Street Journal,* 13 March 2000, A47.

32. Ibid., Other strict constructions, however, have decried this as a yet another example of abusing the due process clause. Michael S. Greve, constitutional scholar at the American Enterprise Institute, says limits on state damage awards, even with an out-state nexus, are an "unconstitutional choice-of-law regime." Michael S. Greve, *The Term the Constitution Died,* AEI, No. 18, August 2003.

33. Brill, *The Court TV Cradle,* 414. "Criminal law involves punitive actions by the government, initiated by prosecutors, to protect people and property from the harmful acts of others...civil law involves lawsuits brought by private individuals and companies to obtain financial compensation or court orders requiring or forbidding specified acts." Criminal law also requires a higher standard to convict: beyond a reasonable doubt, and not just a preponderance of evidence as in civil justice.

34. David Rubenstein, "Lessons Learned from the Tobacco Wars," *Corporate Legal Times*, July 1999, 47.

35. Ibid., 102. As Smith states, "The Court offered no logical or historical justification for abandoning the rule of *Barron v. Baltimore.*"

36. Lineberry, et al, *Government in America,* 55.

37. Smith, *The Constitution,* 124,125. Though the Constitution clearly prohibits the states from impairing the "obligations of contracts," that is generally not how the *Lochner* decisions were justified, as they too relied on a so-called liberty interest in the "due process" clause. Thus, the 1905 decision was short-lived, overruled by *Bunting v. Oregon* in 1917.

38. See *Kelo v. City of New London*, 545 U.S. 469 (2005).

39. See Bill of Rights ratified 1791 (Constitution of the United States).

40. See *Berman v. Parker*, 348 U.S. 26 (1954) and *Poletown Neighborhood Council v. City of Detroit*, 304 N.W. 2d 455 (Michigan: 1981).

41. Levy and Mellor, *The Dirty Dozen,* 167. A number of states have passed ballot initiatives addressing "public use" in eminent domain and even a number of state courts have weighed in by striking down expansive condemnation statutes.

42. Steven J. Eagle, Policy Analysis No. 558, *Cato Institute*, 15 December 2005, 5.

43. Banning, *The Sacred Fire,* 279.

44. In *Lynch v. Household Finance Corp.* 405 U.S.538 (1972), the high court flirted with *Lochner,* expanding the notion of "privacy" to include property rights.

CHAPTER 5

God, Guns, and Gays

PERHAPS NOTHING BRINGS more clarity to the debate over states' rights than those issues swirling around the First and Second Amendments to the United States Constitution. And religious freedom provides a textbook case.

In 1993 Congress passed the Religious Freedom Restoration Act (RFRA) as a response to a Supreme Court decision three years earlier upholding an Oregon penalty for using peyote as part of American Indian worship. RFRA was subsequently used to protect "religious liberty" when the city of Boerne, Texas, denied a construction permit under a local historic preservation ordinance. The controversy arose when the archbishop of San Antonio sought the permit to demolish and rebuild a church within the diocese. When it was denied, the archbishop sued, invoking the RFRA. The Supreme Court finally heard the case and ruled in favor of the local law.[1]

It may be gratifying to see Congress, as it did in RFRA, directly confront the Court over this modern-day shibboleth known as the "independent judiciary." The courts after all are not independent of the Constitution or the people. But neither is Congress. The federal government may not hide behind the First Amendment in order to diminish the states' police power, which is on equal footing with the Bill of Rights.

While legislation may enforce our various liberties, it may not enlarge them. As previously noted, Article I, Section VIII's "necessary and proper clause" does not give "unlimited discretion to Congress."[2] In *Kimel* the Supreme Court properly rejected the use of Section V within the Fourteenth Amendment to likewise enforce law that "is not appropriate legislation."[3]

Sympathy resides with the archbishop who brought the case; local zoning ordinances often strangle freedom of action. But the Court could see ominous trends if it ruled in favor of the RFRA. Could Congress then "protect" religious freedom from state laws prohibiting, say, animal sacrifice, or even worse? What of other nuisance laws protecting property from infringement by the misuse of another's under the guise of worship?

Despite the Court's ruling in *Boerne*, "religious liberty" is expanding under the RFRA. In 2006, the Court unanimously struck down the federal seizure of sacramental tea containing a banned substance from a New Mexico church, based on the law.[4] Even enemy combatants are getting in on the act. Suspected terrorists held at Guantanamo Bay have filed suit alleging violations of their religious liberties under the RFRA. The danger here is doing for "religious liberty" what's been done for "privacy rights;" that is, elevating them to an unrecognizable status and eventually sacrificing the police power of the states on the altar of a federal interpretation of both.

Small-government advocates should applaud decisions like *Boerne* because it represents one of the few instances where the Supreme Court has looked upon something as beyond the national government's enumerated powers. Federalism embraces a healthy skepticism of all federal power, not just a Jeffersonian mistrust of the judiciary. Remember, even when the Court does get it right, as in the *Lopez* case, advocates for limited government must be on the lookout for members of Congress who insist on passing legislation designed to evade the Court's ruling. And it matters little who's in the majority.

As French philosopher Frederic Bastiat once said, "The safest way to make laws respected is to make them respectable."[5] So the proliferation of local zoning laws and city ordinances, often turning ordinary citizens into criminals overnight, represent a legitimate concern for critics of an emerging nanny state. Peter Huber reminds us that the law should not bother itself with all disputes. "Without some sort of legal charter permitting a modest measure of routine public inconvenience or hazard in the pursuit of ordinary business, those who specialize in doing will be perpetually at the mercy of those who specialize in objecting. Judges were not the least bit eager to adjudicate an endless series of these parochial disputes over minor inconveniences. They insisted that a nuisance had to be serious if it was to be considered in court at all."[6] Consequently, libertarians such as Epstein and Glenn Reynolds of the University of Tennessee Law College suggest that states' police power is in fact constitutionally limited.

The "traditional notion was '*sic utere tuo ut alienum non laedas*' or 'use your own property in such a manner as not

to injure that of another.' It was not until much later—
toward the end of the nineteenth century—that the rule was
changed to '*salus popula suprema lex*,' or 'the welfare of the
people is the supreme law.'"[7] Epstein, Reynolds, et al., may
be philosophically correct about the state's prerogative to
"counter various nuisances" being limited by the precedents
of tort law.[8] But there's a difference between what you wish
the law to be and what the law actually is.

Academic colleague McDonald insists the rubric
known as "internal police," as legacy from English common
law, included "not only the definition and punishment of
crimes and the administration of justice but also all matters
concerning the health, manners, morals, safety, and welfare of
the citizenry. Despite the assertions of some anti-Federalists,
the states retained the police powers exclusively."[9] Indeed, it
is hard to imagine a federal limitation on the internal power
of the police, given the myriad of laws already in place by the
colonies at the time of ratification and subsequent adoption
of the Bill of Rights.

It's also difficult to see how even limiting the definition
of the police power to such a degree would prevent the
myriad of ordinances that now exist, given they all pretend to
protect someone from harm done by another. For example,

animals have traditionally been considered property; does that mean you may do with them what you wish, including cruel treatment?

The activists may be right about one thing, however; freedom is sometimes more difficult to define in practice than theory. In any collection of people there exists a tension between liberty and license. Where one ends and the other begins is one of the paramount questions of public policy. It is best answered through what Justice Louis Brandeis called the "laboratories of democracies" rather than one-size-fits-all big government.[10]

These "laboratories" provide the authentic constitutional check on state government because they induce a "competitive federalism between the several states."[11] Critics may fear a race to the bottom as state power grows, but it's a false dichotomy to suggest that choices are between omnipotent local government and "absolute" freedom. Maximum liberty consistent with self-government is more likely to result in a race to the top when people are free to "vote with their feet." The far more dangerous scenario is relying on a more distant authority to safeguard the most basic of liberties—including the right to bear arms.

The confirmation hearing of Justice Sonia Sotomayor

proves the point. Asked by Senator Tom Coburn of Oklahoma whether or not the right of self-defense even existed, she demurred, "That is an abstract question with no meaning to me."[12] For heaven's sake, how then are we to rely on federal judges to apply the Bill of Rights when so many of them refuse to uphold the most fundamental of freedoms as clearly outlined in the Second Amendment?

No doubt, Sotomayor was relying on precedent in *Presser v. Illinois* when she answered the questions. The nineteenth century decision, on appeal from a lower court, upheld a state law forbidding unofficial militias and said the Second Amendment is a "limitation only upon the power of Congress and the national government." [13] She had previously relied upon *Presser* when helping to decide an appeals court decision that restricted the federal government's ability to regulate firearms (but was essentially silent as to whether the states could). Second Amendment advocates pounced on the nominee's hypocrisy—as well they should.[14] After all, given a hundred years worth of applying all sorts of rights upon the states, it seems more than a little inconsistent that the Second Amendment wouldn't also be protected.

Moreover, the nominee seemed to ignore the inevitability of *Dist. of Columbia v. Heller*, which had already established the right to bear arms as individual. So the only legal question left to be decided was whether self-defense is a *fundamental* right guaranteed by a Bill of Rights already incorporated.[15] Logically, the answer had to be yes, and that's what the justices (a few reluctantly) found in *McDonald v. City of Chicago*, decided in the summer of 2010.[16] Justice Scalia, who had long expressed reservations about such holdings, nevertheless "acquiesced" because the "due process" ruling in the decision was "both long established and narrowly limited."[17]

Civil libertarians are pleased with the Court's ruling, but the downside of the landmark decision is its confirmation of the Supreme Court as the sole arbiter of our liberties. The better point, as Justice Scalia opined in *Heller*, is the right to bear arms "existed prior to the formation of the new government under the Constitution.[18] Even *Presser*, while refusing to incorporate the Bill of Rights, also declared that the right of self-defense is not in "any manner dependent upon that instrument for its existence."[19] And in *Robertson v. Baldwin* the Supreme Court asserted "The first ten amendments to the Constitution of the United States...were not intended to lay down any novel principles of government, but simply embodied certain guarantees and immunities which we had inherited from our English ancestors..."[20]

What these cases suggest is that all governments were limited in restricting the inherent right of self-defense whether or not the Bill of Rights is applied to state law.[21] The reason is simple: our rights are preexisting and are not granted by any government, including the states. The Bill of Rights merely acknowledged them and "protected them against Congress' infringement."[22]

When it comes to our most cherished liberties, the question really is whom do you trust to preserve (or at least not infringe) them. As a practical matter, I happen to have more faith in local government. "Nine state constitutional provisions written in the eighteenth century or the first two decades of the nineteenth" guaranteed a right of citizens to bear arms in self-defense.[23] Montana, for instance, is now on record that, should the federal government threaten its citizens' right to bear arms, it would consider that a violation of its compact to enter the union in 1889.[24]

Nevertheless, in *McDonald*, activists from both sides of the fence wanted the Court to go further, overturn *Presser*, and find that certain "rights" were protected by the "privileges and immunities" clause within the Fourteenth Amendment.[25] Though Justice Thomas invoked the clause for his concurring vote, the majority demurred, citing "no need to reconsider the Court's interpretation of the privileges or immunities clause in the *Slaughter-House* cases."[26]

Good thing, because the fault in *Presser's* reasoning was not its refusal to define what "privileges and immunities" states would be forced to recognize—an open-ended invitation for federal micro-management. No, *Presser's* problem was its suggestion that no state may "prohibit the people from keeping and bearing arms" *for the purposes of constituting a militia.*[27]

To the contrary, as *Heller* finally recognized, the right to bear arms is an individual right. The Second Amendment's reference to the "the security of a free state" pertains to individual militia members as a "natural defense of a free country" or the "security of a polity" in eighteenth century discourse.[28] In fact, the very *raison d'être* of the Bill of Rights was to protect the individual from federal encroachment.[29] So it is not whether individuals have an inherent right of self-defense, they most certainly do. All our other liberties are ancillary to the basic right of self-preservation.[30]

The danger lies in the activists' newfound zeal to reinterpret the "privileges and immunities" clause, providing yet another avenue for federal interference at the expense of states' rights. Imagine, virtually any law passed by a state legislature could conceivably be in violation of someone's "privileges and immunities"—which these days apparently includes the right to a government subsidy. Yet more than a few libertarians (with whom I usually agree) suggest this one clause actually "meant to rewrite...the relationship between the federal government and the states."[31] The history of the clause suggests otherwise.

The Articles of Confederation proclaimed "to secure and perpetuate mutual friendship and intercourse among the people of the different states in this union...all privileges and immunities of free citizens in the several states; and the people of each state shall have free ingress and regress to and from any other state and shall enjoy therein all the privileges of trade and commerce, subject to the same duties, impositions and restrictions as the inhabitants thereof respectively."[32]

In *Abbot v. Bayley* (1827), the Massachusetts Court noted that the "privileges and immunities secured to the people of each state in every other state can be applied only in case of removal from one state to another...That they have the privileges and immunities of citizens; that is they...may take and hold real estate; and may, according to the laws of such state, eventually enjoy the rights of citizenship..."[33]

Translation: the original intent of the "privileges and immunities" clause was to guarantee that nonresident "citizens" (as opposed to "persons" in the "due process" clause) of a particular state had the same rights of a state's own inhabitants, including for example the right to travel that is now "firmly embedded in our jurisprudence."[34]

It is in that context that Article IV, Section 2, of the Constitution, which reads, "The citizens of each state shall be entitled to all privileges and immunities of citizens in the several states," has thus been interpreted.[35] Berger notes that court decisions from the founding to the early twentieth century clearly make "manifest that it was drawn with reference to the corresponding clause of the Articles of Confederation and was intended to perpetuate its limitations."[36]

The much maligned *Slaughter-House* decision—written just a few years after ratification in 1873—also interpreted the intent of the clause narrowly. "The entire domain of the privileges and immunities of citizens of the states," wrote Justice Miller, "lay within the constitutional power and legislative power of the states and outside that of the federal government" and he added, "there can be but little question that the purposes of both these provisions is the same, and that the privileges and immunities intended are the same in each."[37]

Critics of the decision note the minority's strong dissent that suggested the Court's majority was overturning the supposed will of the Fourteenth Amendment. Yet no scholar disputes the history of the clause itself or the fact that its constitutional antecedent did nothing to diminish the sovereignty of the states. As Berger notes, how could those who initially authored the "privileges and immunities" clause in Article IV intend for it to incorporate a federal Bill of Rights that did not textually exist at the time of its original drafting?[38]

Moreover, Congress could have taken subsequent action at several points to "correct" *Slaughter-House* (such as removing appellate jurisdiction or further amending the Constitution) had the Court's decision been so far removed from the drafter's intentions or plain wording of the Fourteenth Amendment. It did not.

In fact, the Amendment's primary purpose was to constitutionalize the Civil Rights Act of 1866—a legislative response to local reluctance to fully emancipate freed blacks.[39] Historians from the time of ratification well into the twentieth century confirm that "virtually every speech in the debates on the amendment—Republican and Democrat alike—said or agreed that the Amendment was designed to embody or incorporate the Civil Rights Act."[40]

The Black Codes had imposed harsh limits on property rights, including bound apprenticeship and the denial to contract. The rights of self-defense, echoed in a Mississippi law that "banned any negro or mulatto from having firearms," were also in the crosshairs of the Act.[41] Senator James Nye, arguing for the legislation, declared that blacks have an "equal right to protection and to keep and bear arms for self-defense."[42] The clause meant that states could no longer disarm blacks without disarming the white majority, which was unthinkable at the time.

It is this aspect of removing *unequal* treatment and providing newly freed slaves with the same "privileges and immunities" as white men that was the driving force behind the Civil War Amendments.

Thaddeus Stevens, another proponent of the Fourteenth Amendment, made clear that the thrust of the Civil Rights Acts and its authorization under the Fourteenth Amendment was to start the process of eliminating discrimination by state governments on account of race.[43]

Section 1 of the bill took dead aim by declaring that "there shall be no discrimination in civil rights or immunities... on account of race...but the inhabitants of every state shall have the same right to make and enforce contracts, to sue, be parties and give evidence, to inherit purchase, lease, sell, hold and convey real and personal property, and to full and equal benefit to all laws and proceedings for the security of person and property..."[44]

McDonald says, "The main purpose of the first section of the Fourteenth Amendment, which contains the privileges and immunities clause, was to establish Negro citizenship, contrary to the *Dred Scott* decision. But the section explicitly distinguished between citizens of the United States and citizens of a specific state. The privileges and immunities clause prohibited states from abridging rights arising from national citizenship, but not those arising from state citizenship. Those that derived from national citizenship and were common to all were few, including the right to travel to the seat of government, to transact business with it and seek its protection, to have access to seaports, and to be protected in one's life, liberty, and property on the high seas."[45]

In the wake of *Dred Scott*—which had denied freedom for those who had traveled from slave state to free—it is this dual citizenship which gave real meaning to "privileges and immunities" for emancipated blacks. "It was precisely because Article IV(2) did not protect the resident emancipated black," according to Berger, "that the privileges and immunities clause of the Fourteenth Amendment was made applicable to citizens of the United States."[46] Essentially, it amounted to little more than a restatement of liberty manifest in English common law, but now applicable for all U.S. citizens, and exemplified by "due process" in tribunals and "equal protection." Only by understanding the limited scope of the clause itself can one assert a proper right of national citizenship that transcends the states.[47]

But even the Civil Rights Act itself was thought too expansive by some of the most prominent legislators. Representative John Bingham (draftsman of Section One of the Fourteenth Amendment) took exception to the bill's scope and questioned whether it would "strike down by Congressional enactment every state constitution which makes a discrimination on account of race..."[48] Because a number of Northern states denied the right to vote for blacks, including Bingham's Ohio, framers of the Civil War Amendments felt it necessary to construct a companion amendment almost two years later in order to preserve voting rights.[49] This doesn't suggest a very broad reading of "privileges and immunities."

The ratification debates make it fairly clear that the framers of the Civil War Amendments had little appetite for threatening the power reserved to their respective states. As Bingham said, referring once again to the civil rights legislation, "Now what does this bill propose? To reform the whole criminal and civil code of every state government?"[50]

Well, yes, if you subscribe to the legal activism of the modern era. In fact, it is hard to actually figure out if any state law could survive an expansive view of "privileges and immunities." Some observers suggest the federal judiciary exists to prevent state legislatures from interfering where no "third party can be heard to complain that his rights are violated by those performing the proscribed acts."[51] Are we then to assume that partial-birth abortion, physician-assisted suicide, prostitution, and same-sex marriage qualify as constitutional rights?

The Supreme Court has come awfully close. In *Lawrence v. Texas*, the majority found a constitutional right to sodomy, overturning a Georgia law that had been upheld just seventeen years earlier.[52] Now, as already mentioned, there are good reasons to oppose so-called "consensual" crime statutes. The laws are seldom enforced and most people agree that the police probably have better things to do, but it's a matter for the individual states to sort out. Yet in *Lawrence*, Justice Anthony Kennedy, writing for the majority, somewhat miraculously discovered "rights" based on the concept of one's own existence, whatever that means, and further held that the "right to privacy" means a constitutional right to sex.

If this is so, then how is it that a state may regulate the agreed-upon (consensual) rate of interest between debtor and creditor, the wages between employee and employer? After all, privacy is privacy, whether in economic affairs or those of the heart. The fact is: there may be a stronger case for the banning of sex acts in the name of public health than there is for the myriad of state usury laws, though both as a matter of policy (not law) are unwise.

Justice Sandra Day O'Connor, usually a more reliable voice for federalism, wrote a concurring opinion in *Lawrence* that declared the Texas law unconstitutional on equal protection grounds (a harbinger of things to come). An odd view, considering the Texas law applied to everyone—black, white, male, female. Nevertheless, the constitutional damage was done and it took the Massachusetts Supreme Court just about two paragraphs before they cited *Lawrence* in ordering its state legislature to endorse same-sex marriage in the Bay state.[53]

The first federal trial over a state ban on gay marriage began working its way through the federal courts in California during the summer of 2010. Proposition 8, passed by ballot initiative in 2008 is being challenged by gay couples claiming the California constitution now discriminates against "the right to marry and the right to equal protection under the law."[54] Of course, there is no constitutional "right" to marry, as family law has been traditionally left to the states. Moreover, Congress had invoked a "public policy exception" to the Full Faith and Credit Clause in 1996 when President Bill Clinton signed the Defense of Marriage Act (DOMA), thus providing grounds upon which any state may deny recognition of a same-sex union—even if performed in another state.[55] The vast majority of states have already opted to pass traditional marriage laws as a result. Seeing the legislative losses mount, activists have predictably shifted the fight to the courts. And that is where the battle has thus far been fought.

Iowa, for example, had its Defense of Marriage Act (DOMA) struck down in a bizarre ruling. The state's high court initially asserted that state law must be applied equally to everyone who may wish to marry someone from the opposite sex. So far so good, but the court then leaps to an arbitrary judgment by finding that gay "plaintiffs are similarly situated compared to heterosexual persons" with respect to purposes of the law governing marriage.[56]

A more fanciful definition of legal uniformity could not be found. Obviously the explicit purpose of DOMA made clear that same-sex marriage was not "similarly situated" to a heterosexual union. Can there really be any doubt as to the intention of the legislation? Furthermore, the law itself makes no direct classification on the basis of race (the real intent of the Civil War Amendments), gender, or even sexual orientation as long as civil marriage consists of two individuals of the opposite sex. That is, anyone may marry under the law in question.

The Court got around this by arguing that plaintiffs need not be identical, or even in identical circumstances, for Iowa's test of legal uniformity to apply. Otherwise "nearly every equal protection claim could be run aground under a threshold analysis...rather," the Court asserts, "equal protection demands that the law itself must be equal."[57] This is breathtaking activism.

Gay couples are no more discriminated against than

the polygamist, the drug user, or the loan shark. Local governments regulate all sorts of behavior, for good or ill. Taxpayers fund the public school system even if they don't have children or if they send their children to private schools. While that sort of discrimination may not be a good idea, it's not unconstitutional. The only requirement is that any law be applied equally for individuals in similar circumstances—even for those who find themselves in, say, higher tax brackets than their neighbors.[58] Come to think of it, the Iowa Smokefree Air Act of 2008 clearly discriminates against smokers and is therefore unconstitutional using the Court's analysis. That's absurd as long as the law covers everyone equally who chooses to smoke.

The lesson here is that, even on the state level, courts are opting for policy preferences, not sound judicial decisions. But unless DOMA itself is overturned in the federal courts, the effects of these wayward state decisions, thankfully, have limited effect. It is up to the people in those states to correct their judicial deficiencies.

The larger issue is the gulf between the courts and the people. By 2010, five states, not counting the District of Columbia, have legalized same-sex marriage—most through court-imposed rulings, none by popular vote. On the other hand, thirty-one states (all who have put it to a vote) have rejected same-sex marriage on state-wide ballot initiatives, with liberal Maine even repealing their same-sex marriage law. Regardless of how one feels on the issue, a disconnect of this magnitude between judges and voters is of troubling concern.

CHAPTER 5 NOTES

1. See *Boerne v. Flores* (1997).

2. Banning, *The Sacred Fire,* 327. Madison said, "Whatever meaning the clause may have, none can be admitted that it would give an unlimited discretion to Congress."

3. *Kimel v. Florida Board of Regents,* 528 U.S. 62 (2000).

4. *Gonzales v. O Centro Espirita Beneficente Uniao do Vegetal, 546 U.S. 418 (2006).*

5. Frederic Bastiat, *The Law,* 1848 (Whittier: reprinted by Constructive Action, Inc., 1964) 17. What's respectable? In the law, it's what's acceptable. For example, negligence cases are sometimes adjudicated by comparing the defendant's actions with that of what the majority of his or her fellow citizens might do in similar situations.

6. Huber, *Liability,* 63. *De minimus non curat lex* was the rule—"the law does not concern itself with trifles."

7. Glenn Harlan Reynolds, conversation and written fax with author, 27 January 1997. To be fair, it should be noted that libertarians don't deny a role for the states' police power in those cases where someone must draw the line in criminal law.

8. *Village of Euclid v. Amber Realty Co.* 272 U.S. 365 (1926). Nuisance has been historically defined as "a condition or situation that interferes with the use or enjoyment of property," according to *Black's Law Dictionary*. Practically speaking, it's not so easily identified; in *Euclid*, the Supreme Court said, "A nuisance may merely be a right thing in the wrong place, like a pig in a parlor instead of a barnyard."

9. McDonald, *Novus Ordo Seclorum*, 288.

10. Brandeis' notion came in dissent of the Court's opinion striking down an Oklahoma law favoring a local monopoly. While his economics may have been askew, his view of the republic was more accurate. "It is one of the happy incidents of the federal system that a single courageous state may, if its citizens choose, serve as a laboratory; and try novel social and economic experiments without risk to the rest of the country." See *New State Ice Co. v. Liebmann* 285 U.S. 262 (1932).

11. Thomas Dye, author and professor at Florida State University, has been credited with the concept. Public choice theorists, such as James Buchanan, have also greatly refined the issue.

12. http://features.csmonitor.com/politics/2009/07/15/sotomayor-dodges-gun-rights-questions/ (Accessed July 2010)

13. Clayton E. Cramer, *For The Defense of Themselves and The State*, Praeger: Westport 1994) 126. *Presser v. Illinois* 116 U.S. 252 (1886). On appeal from a lower court, the Supreme Court upheld a state law forbidding unofficial militias and said the Second Amendment is "a limitation only upon the power of Congress and the national government..." This decision was a follow on to *U.S. v. Cruikshank* 92 U.S. 542 (1875), which ten years earlier ruled in a similar manner.

14. Second Amendment, United States Constitution, 1791.The Second Amendment reads, "A well regulated Militia, being necessary to the security of a free state, the right of the people to keep and bear arms, shall not be infringed..."

15. *District of Columbia v. Heller,* 554 U.S. ___ 2008. Justice Scalia's majority opinion in *Dist. of Columbia v. Heller*, outlines the literal and theoretical history of the meaning of the right of self-defense within the Second Amendment in striking down a *federal* handgun ban. Though a precursor for incorporating Second Amendment rights to the states in *McDonald*, the Court nonetheless upheld the D.C. Circuit Court's view of a "natural right of self-preservation" independent of law.

16. Jess Bravin, "Handgun Case Creates Odd Alliances," *Wall Street Journal*, 10 February 2010. See *McDonald v. City of Chicago*, 561 U.S. ____ (2010) Justice Scalia had previously written that "the Second Amendment as a guarantee that the federal government would not interfere with the right of the people to keep and bear arms. Of course, properly understood, it is no limitation upon arms control by the states."

17. Review & Outlook, "Five Gun Salute," *Wall Street Journal*, 29 June 2010.

18. Justice Scalia's majority opinion in *Dist. of Columbia v. Heller*, 554 U.S. ____ 2008.

19. Cramer, *For The Defense*, 125,126. *U.S. v. Cruikshank* 92 U.S. 542 (1875) as quoted by Cramer.

20. Cramer, *For The Defense*, 143.

21. *Nunn v. State*, 1 Ga. 243 (1846). Long before the Civil War Amendments, the Georgia State Supreme Court in *Nunn* applied the federal bill of rights (also see Goodwin) to strike a Georgia statute banning openly carried weapons, but also legal tradition. While the Georgia court's decision properly demonstrates the power of the several states to uphold our liberties, it too declared that state constitutions "confer no new rights on the people which did not belong to them before," while at the same time stating that "the presumption is in favor of every legislative act" when there are constitutional questions, including restrictions on concealed weapons that did not diminish the natural right to self-defense.

22. Cramer, *For The Defense*, 126.

23. *District of Columbia v. Heller*, 554 U.S. ____ 2008, 11.

24. Radley Balko, "Republic of Montana," *Reason Magazine*, June 2008: www.reason.com/news/show/126063.html. (Accessed December 2009)

25. "No State shall make or enforce any law which shall abridge the privileges and immunities of citizens of the United States," See the *Constitution of the United States* (1787).

26. McDonald v. City of Chicago, 561 U.S. ___ (2010), SCOTUS syllabus 5.

27. Cramer, *For The Defense,* 130.

28. See Scalia's reference to constitutional historian Joseph Story in his majority opinion in *District of Columbia v. Heller,* 554 U.S. ___ (2008) 24.

29. Lysander Spooner, *An Essay on the Trial by Jury* (www.barefootsworld. net/trial01.html, 1852) 17. (Accessed April 2010) "This right of resistance is recognized by the Constitution of the United States, as a strictly legal and constitutional right. It is recognized, first by the provision that 'trial of all crimes, except in cases of impeachment, shall be by jury'—that is, by the country, and not by the government; secondly, by the provision that 'the right of the people to keep and bear arms shall not be infringed.'"

30. Thomas Jefferson to John Calvin, 1810. ME 12:418, Charlottesville (VA): University of Virginia Library, Electronic Text Center; 1995; c1999 http:// etext.lib.virginia. edu/jefferson/ quotations/index.html. (Accessed May 2002) Jefferson once said that officers of the law may have a duty "to assume authorities beyond," adding that "a strict observance of the written law is doubtless one of the high duties of a good citizen, but it is not the highest. The laws of necessity, of self-preservation, of saving our country when in danger, are of higher obligation."

31. Kimberly Shankman and Roger Pilon, "Reviving the Privileges and Immunities Clause," Policy Analysis No. 326, *Cato Institute*, 23 November 1998, 28.

32. See Articles of Confederation, 1781

33. Berger, *The Fourteenth Amendment,* 34.

34. *Saenz v. Roe*, 526 U.S. 489 (1999). Justice John Paul Stevens' majority opinion in *Saenz*—which held that states may not discriminate in disbursing welfare benefits for new residents—may or may not be directly applicable to the right to travel. However, that fundamental right, mentioned in the Articles of Confederation, but not specifically in the Constitution is consistent with a more traditional view of "privileges and immunities."

35. See Constitution of the United States, 1787.

36. Berger, *The Fourteenth Amendment*, 93, 94.

37. *Slaughter-House Cases* 83 U.S. 36 (1873).

38. Stephen Wermiel, "Justice Scalia Often Turns to Tradition, Historical Practice in Making Rulings," *The Wall Street Journal*, 20 May 1991, 2A. This attachment to history and tradition gives the founding documents real meaning. And properly so. We know theoretically, for instance, that the rights of free speech must be weighed against competing rights. But how else do we know that the First Amendment offers no protection for, say, slander? Because it never has. We have defined speech through the appropriate prism of history. It is to this original intent that Justices like Antonin Scalia so often defer. By first assessing the "text of the Constitution, but when words of the Constitution don't provide an answer, he examines the history of court precedents, known as case law, sometimes even predating the Constitution."

39. McDonald, *States' Rights*, (2000) 212.

40. Quotation from Howard Jay Graham, an early advocate of an abolitionist reading of the Fourteenth Amendment. See also Charles Fairman, Alexander Bickel and Raoul Berger, *The Fourteenth Amendment*, 7, 22, 23.

41. Akhil Reed Amar and Les Adams, *The Bill of Rights Primer*, (Birmingham: Palladium Press: 2002) 249.

42. Ibid.

43. Lino A. Graglia, "Order in the Court," *National Review*, 24 November 1997, 48.

44. Berger, *The Fourteenth Amendment,* 24, 25.

45. McDonald, *States' Right,* 219. The first part of *Dred Scott* dismissed the suit in federal court because slaves had no right to such action due to a lack of national citizenship. The *Slaughter-House* cases merely said that the "right" to labor as butcher is or is not protected by the states and not the federal government.

46. Berger, *The Fourteenth Amendment,* 94.

47. Shankman and Pilon, "Reviving the Privileges," 24. Justice Miller for the majority in *Slaughter-House* wrote that the amendment was not intended "as a protection to the citizen of a state against the legislative power of his own state," though critics contend that "Miller held that the clause creates distinct citizenship's—state and national, each conferring its own set of rights—and that the Privileges and Immunities Clause protects only rights of national citizenship, which he then read narrowly."

48. Berger, *The Fourteenth Amendment,* 25, 26, 28, 29.

49. The Fifteenth Amendment to the Constitution was ratified in 1870 and reads that the "right of the citizens of the United States to vote shall not be denied or abridged by the United States or by any State on account of race, color, or previous condition of servitude." See Constitution of the United States.

50. Berger, *The Fourteenth Amendment,* 28, 75.

51. Roger Pilon, "The Complexities of 'Unfair Discrimination,'" *The Wall Street Journal,* 13 December 2002, A17.

52. The majority's opinion in *Lawrence v. Texas,* 539 U.S. 558 (2003) overruled *Bowers v. Hardwick* in 1986.

53.   *Goodridge v. Dept. of Public Health,* 798 N.E. 2nd 941 (Mass, 2003).

54. Karen Gullo, "California Gay Marriage Ban on Trial in San Francisco," *Business Week.* 11 January 2010. http://www.businessweek.com/news/2010-01-11/california-gay-marriage-ban-on-trial-in-san-francisco-update3-.html (Accessed February 2010)

55. Article IV, Section 1 of the Constitution reads: "Full Faith and Credit shall be given in each state to the public's acts, records, and judicial proceedings of every other state. And the Congress may by general laws prescribe the manner in which such acts, records, and proceedings shall be proved, and the effect thereof." See Constitution of the United States, Philadelphia, 1787.

56. The Iowa court ruled on the state's own equal protection clause, but also noted developments coming out of the *Lawrence* case. *Varnum v. Brien,* 763 N.W. 2d 862, (Iowa, 2009).

57. Ibid.

58. In *Federal Communications Commission v. Beach,* (1993) the court said that when it comes to economic regulations if "there is any conceivable state of facts that could provide a rational basis," they would uphold the classifications. But if we are to apply equal protection broadly enough to include same-sex marriage, a consistent reading would also have to ban distinctions based on economic standing. Here again, another example of judicial arbitrariness when it comes to property rights. *Federal Communications Commission v Beach,* 508 U.S. 307 (1993).

CHAPTER 6

General Welfare and Interstate Commerce

PERHAPS THE MOST CONTENTIOUS detail in the Obama administration's massive one-size-fits-all healthcare plan is the individual mandate for citizens to buy health insurance. Beyond the economics of such a Herculean task, the federal government has never before instructed citizens to buy a particular product, which is one reason why it is being challenged in court. Senator John Ensign (R-NV) raised a constitutional point of order on the issue during the Senate debate, citing a 1994 Congressional Budget Office analysis that said, "The government has never required people to buy any good or service as a condition of lawful residence in the United States."[1] Senator Coburn, once again at a Senate confirmation hearing, asked President Obama's second nominee to the high court, Elena Kagen, whether the federal government could write a bill demanding that Americans "eat three vegetables and three fruits every day," clearly referring to the president's healthcare requirements.[2] The nominee avoided giving a direct answer.

At the time of this writing, fourteen state attorneys general have filed suit against the federal government, challenging the requirement of its citizens to purchase health insurance.[3] The majority of the remaining states also have similar legislation pending.

Though proponents of the healthcare bill cite the supremacy of federal law (without acknowledging that it must first be constitutional), there is little doubt that a Tenth Amendment showdown is brewing. In fact, because purchasing health insurance from a local broker is likely divorced from its effects on interstate commerce, the administration may not get far relying on the commerce power to enforce such a requirement.[4] Requiring interstate commerce is not the same as regulating it. "There's no provision in the Constitution that allows for anybody to be forced to do something when there's no commerce, no action, you're just sitting there," says Florida Attorney General Bill McCollum.[5]

For his part, the president suggests a federal fine for refusing to buy health insurance is no different than requirements to buy automobile insurance, "and if you don't, you're subject to some penalty."[6] But when states do this, they are attaching a regulation onto something that an individual chooses to do. Besides, they have much wider authority under the police power.

Washington's healthcare mandate offers no choice, and is far beyond the reach of federal power anyway. If Congress could merely cite interstate commerce for whatever act it chose to pass, an amendment to the Constitution would never have been necessary to ban "the manufacture, sale or transportation of intoxicating liquors" throughout the United States during Prohibition.[7] Perhaps that's why the administration has already signaled its intent to rely on its power to spend as it wishes under the general welfare clause—arguing that the federal plan is essentially a healthcare subsidy program with certain strings attached. Intuitively, most people see this as a constitutional stretch as well.

The "power to lay and collect taxes, duties, imposts and excises, to pay the debts and provide for the common defense and general welfare" has been perhaps the most abused and frequently cited phrase for expanding federal power in the nation's history.[8] And it remains the catchall for any spending program a politician desires for the benefit of lifetime tenure. Ironically, the notion of "general welfare" was probably vetted more clearly by the framers than any other. When Alexander Hamilton (a strict constructionist by twenty-first century standards) questioned the limits of general welfare in his Report on Manufacturers in 1791, he was forthrightly rebuked by both Jefferson and Madison.[9]

According to Dr. Mortimer Adler's *We Hold These Truths*, "Thomas Jefferson was so disturbed by this statement in Hamilton's report that he discussed it with George Washington, who was then president, saying that the people were compelled by it to consider whether they were living under a limited or unlimited government."[10] Jefferson maintained that the clause, found in the preamble as well, was not designed to subvert the safeguards of the Constitution. It was a statement of purpose, not a license for Congress "to do any act they please, which might be for the good of the Union" because that "would render all the preceding and subsequent enumerations of power completely useless. It would reduce the whole instrument to a single phrase..."[11]

Madison addressed the issue in "Federalist 41," noting that "general welfare" was used in explicit conjunction with "common defense" and they were "not even separated by a longer pause than a semicolon...for what purpose could the enumeration of particular powers be inserted, if these and all others were meant to be included in the preceding general power?"[12] Consequently he denied Hamilton's report a hearing in Congress because the Constitution was "not a general grant, out of which particular powers are excepted—it is a grant of particular powers only, leaving the general mass in other hands."[13]

Unfortunately, starting with the Progressive Era and Theodore Roosevelt, things began to unravel. The trust-busting populist was every bit the big-government liberal as his Democratic successors would turn out to be, though he is still admired by misguided Republicans. T.R. campaigned for a graduated income tax, even suggesting that a man is entitled to his property "only so long as the gaining represents benefit to the community."[14] Worse, Teddy's populist demagoguery laid the groundwork for his distant cousin, Franklin Roosevelt, to radically alter the economic landscape in the 1930s.

Since then the Constitution has become a general

grant of unlimited federal power, especially in the arena of economic affairs. FDR's New Deal turned out to be the equivalent of a constitutional revolution—without ever amending the document. While much of the legislation, such as the Railroad Retirement Act, the Bituminous Coal Conservation Act, etc. was originally rebuffed (and nearly all of it would never have passed just a few years earlier), an unrelenting FDR and a compliant, if not activist, Supreme Court permanently enlarged the scope of federal power.[15]

A seminal moment in redefining federal power took place, appropriately enough, at a cocktail party in 1934. The Roosevelt administration, still searching for a way to expand the central government, got its answer from Justice Harlan Stone when he whispered into the ear of Labor Secretary Frances Perkins, "The taxing power, my dear, is all you need."[16] By linking the taxing and spending power to general welfare, the administration had the opening it was looking for. The Court soon reversed itself on a number of issues, and the New Deal was born.

A couple years later in *U.S. v. Butler*—though striking down the subsidy schemes of the Agricultural Adjustment Act of 1933—the justices defined the tax and spending power broadly, establishing that Congress' power "to authorize expenditure of public moneys for public purposes is not limited by the direct grants of legislative power found in the Constitution."[17] Adding fuel to the fire, the justices remarkably claimed, "The clause confers a power separate and distinct from those later enumerated...and Congress consequently has a substantive power to tax and to appropriate, limited only by the requirement that it shall be exercised to provide for the general welfare of the United States."[18]

Hence, a slew of agricultural price controls and set-aside programs were swiftly enacted, and the carving out of monopolies for favored industries supplied with politically connected organized labor were suddenly found to be constitutional. More devastating, any citizen may plausibly be bound by a federal rule (the feds may regulate that which they subsidize) or even a tax as long as it's part of a federal program. Programs, according to *Butler*, that apparently have no constitutional boundaries.

Conditions attached to every federal transportation dollar, for instance, have resulted in unprecedented intrusion into state matters concerning local speed limits, seat belt use, and alcohol consumption. "Obamacare" (as the health bill has come to be known) continues the trend by requiring the states to spend massive amounts on new Medicaid recipients (if they want any of their federal taxes back). Is it really any wonder why the administration feels it can require people to purchase health insurance—and fine them if they don't?

Of course, the apologists for national healthcare must make some gargantuan assumptions for the plan to pass constitutional muster. First, they must pretend the general welfare clause is an unlimited grant of power. It is not. Second, proponents must assert that the individual mandate is not "actually a mandate...it is a tax," levied against those who don't purchase a premium.[19] Finally, they are forced to claim the whole scheme actually lowers overall healthcare costs; hence the general welfare test is somehow "easily satisfied."[20] Huh?

This, my friends, amounts to a constitutional *coup d'état*.

Even if you believe that Washington can tie funding to federal regulations, the latter much have some relation to the program at hand. The feds cannot attach an unconstitutional condition, such as the suspension of free speech, to funding for roads. In *South Dakota v. Dole*, the Court suggested that these sorts of regulations must be "reasonably related to the purpose of the federal program," but inscrutably went on to uphold, according to dissenting Justice O'Connor, the "establishment of a minimum drinking age of twenty-one" to funds appropriated for "interstate highway construction."[21]

Suppose that Washington rules are tangentially related to a federal program; they still violate the tenets of federalism if the programs enacted under Article 1, Section 8, have no limits. Federal gasoline taxes, collected at the local pump, are to be returned to the states only if they do exactly as the feds wish (e.g., the building of mass transit lines and bike paths). This is legal extortion.

The point is that so much of Washington's power is attributable to unconstitutional federal spending, of which total annual outlays are now approaching an astonishing four trillion dollars annually.[22] The tax and regulatory burden is so consolidated in D.C. that states have become an afterthought when it comes to fiscal policy. For instance, federal grants for state and local government have grown to over 800 annually.[23] Outlays for state and local grants have increased to nearly $500 billion per year, a seventy-three percent increase in just the last decade.[24] Without rediscovering the limits of federal spending (and general welfare), there may be little hope in curtailing the federal Leviathan. Indeed, the notion of a constitutional entitlement has become so ingrained that removing funding for anyone seems next to impossible when coupled with activist judges. The left-wing group, ACORN, whose members are under investigation for everything from voter registration fraud to providing questionable tax-planning tips to prostitutes, has sued the government for denying them a federal grant, claiming it amounts to a "bill of attainder."[25] Even though Congress has always decided on whom to fund, a federal judge actually found in ACORN's favor.

Ronald Reagan was one of the few contemporary politicians who tried to warn us, at least rhetorically. He saw it coming as early as 1964 when he said, "The Founding Fathers knew a government can't control the economy without controlling the people. And they knew when a government sets out to do that; it must use force and coercion to achieve its purpose."[26] Reagan, more than any other modern president, understood the framers' skepticism of big government, even if he was unable to entirely fulfill their vision. The aging president used to joke that he remembered the history so well because he was there.

A good line, but a serious understanding of the founding framework is crucial to this debate. You might recall that the Philadelphia delegates in 1787 never did have explicit authority from their respective states to do much more than revamp the Articles of Confederation. Any attempt at consolidating power in a new central government would have been seen as essentially a coup.[27] Nevertheless, big-government types often point to the founders' advocacy for a strong central authority.

But as we have seen, even federalists had no plans to allow the new government to interfere with "the overwhelming burden of political responsibility" that "would still be carried by the states" in their nascent system of divided government.[28] Madison's proposal for a Congressional veto of state law is often cited by big government apologists, but it was likely motivated by his interest in a more "'perfect freedom' of commerce."[29] Calling it an "indication of how far he wished to go toward a consolidation of authority" is "a serious mistake," according to scholar Lance Banning.[30]

Regardless, the veto idea was summarily dropped in negotiations at the Constitutional Convention.[31] But it's fair to say at some point Madison became increasingly worried about local interference in the ability of Virginians to "find sufficient outlets for the products of their work" among the several states, as well as with foreign nations.[32] Robust commercial trade may have been foremost in the minds of many of the framers.

The commerce clause had been traditionally interpreted as to ensure such activity. But instead of ensuring a free trade among the several states, the interstate commerce clause has become yet another vehicle in the arsenal of judicial activists for interference in the states where none is plainly warranted.[33] It's somewhat ironic, if not sad, that property rights themselves have become the victim of a commerce clause ostensibly intended to enhance them.

In fact, Chief Justice Stone's opinion in 1938's *United States v. Carolene Products* firmly established the legal fiction of two separate standards of review—one for property rights and one for infringement upon those "discrete and insular minorities...which may call for a correspondingly more searching judicial inquiry."[34] And once again, we see a selective application of human rights and a marked departure from Supreme Court precedent. Just a few years earlier the Court openly defied Roosevelt's New Deal nonsense in *Schechter Poultry Corp. v. United States*.[35]

In that case, the administration's National Industrial Recovery Act of 1933 took the illiberal approach that power over commerce included federal price controls (and protection for the well connected) and labor regulations. The Live Poultry Code of the act, with maximum workweek limits and the right to organize, "applied to slaughterhouse operators who took possession of the goods after they had been shipped in interstate commerce."[36] Federal inspectors descended on one of the victims of the legislation, ALA Schechter, a small shop in Brooklyn, and found the violations they were looking for, indicting the Schecter brothers on sixty counts of workweek and minimum wage violations.[37]

You might wonder how the federal government (as opposed to state authorities) could prosecute a business who sold to local butchers for local customers. The traditional view was that once a product has arrived at a local place of business, the interstate transaction is complete. Any further activity within a state had no federal nexus. For the same reason that trade between foreign nations or Indian tribes gave the federal government no power to regulate commerce within those jurisdictions. A unanimous Court in *Schechter* agreed. "Defendants do not sell poultry in interstate commerce," declared Chief Justice Hughes, "Extraordinary conditions may call for extraordinary remedies. But the argument necessarily stops short of an attempt to justify action which lies outside the sphere of constitutional authority."[38]

The Roosevelt administration was undeterred and with case after case challenged the limits of federal power. Finally, in *West Coast Hotel v. Parish*, property rights came crashing down under the weight of an obsequious bench of "nine old men," capitulating to a threat by FDR to pack the Court if his New Deal legislation wasn't upheld. "Protection of property was a major casualty of the revolution of 1937," says federal judge Janice Rogers Brown.[39] Though the Court had previously struck down even local labor laws as a violation of contractual liberty, in *West Coast Hotel* it embraced a Washington state minimum wage statute and in the process signaled that most of the New Deal would now be upheld.[40] It came to be known as the "switch in time that saved nine."

Naturally, it didn't end there. In *United States v. Darby*, a federal minimum wage was established when the Court upheld the unprecedented Fair Labor Standards Act passed in 1938.[41] Jettisoning any pretense of federalist principles, the Court wrote, "It is no longer open to question that the fixing of a minimum wage is within the legislative power and the bare fact of its existence is not a denial of due process under the Fifth more than under the Fourteenth Amendment."[42] Mandatory family leave and a myriad of federal regulations—which could have easily been handled solely by the states—have followed.

Of course, FDR's bizarre interpretation of interstate

commerce had the simple effect of making any commerce, intrastate or interstate, subject to the hand of his regulators. By 1942 the transformation was so complete that the Court decided that "commerce power was not confined in its exercise to the regulation of commerce among the states. It extends to those activities intrastate which affect interstate commerce..."[43] In *Wickard v. Filburn* the justices ruled that a compulsory federal quota actually applied to a farmer who, far from engaging in interstate commerce, was growing wheat for his own consumption.[44]

Not surprisingly, the commerce clause now serves as yet another justification for expanding federal power. Even contracts between two citizens of the same state are no match for activists who wish to rewrite (not enforce) agreements between private parties—voluntary arrangements that were once protected when "liberty to contract" was part of "due process" protection during the *Lochner* era.

A few libertarians long for such a return to *Lochner*, noting it makes little difference which level of government overreaches on such affairs. They advocate a different sort of judicial activism, having the federal courts strike down state and local laws that purportedly fall "outside the police power."[45] Epstein cites *Nebbia v. New York*, among other cases, that allowed New York to regulate a minimum retail price for milk. The deleterious consequences of such silly price controls should be obvious to those familiar with the laws of supply and demand. But the legal question is not whether the Court can correct such glaring deficiencies in economics; it is, rather, whether they have the power to. To be fair, these activists on the right who call for an end to "judicial passivity" at least have philosophical consistency on their side. When it comes to freedom, they make no false distinctions between political rights and property rights. But the point of the founders' federalism was to rely on the national government to guard against foreign threats—not those ostensibly coming from state and local law.

Besides, is it not a logical contradiction to enlarge the power of the federal government in the name of weakening oppressive state governments? The critics' faith in a judiciary that routinely upholds the diminution of property rights through federal law seems more than a bit misplaced. Rep. Bingham himself, one of principal draftsmen of the Fourteenth Amendment, said, "The citizens must rely on the state for their protection."[46]

We simply wouldn't be talking about many of these errant court decisions had Congress not passed legislation far beyond the enumerated powers of the Constitution in the first place. A perfect example is the bill introduced by Rep. James Oberstar and Senator Russ Feingold designed to implement something that the Supreme Court had already specified as unconstitutional.[47] When Michigan land owners had filled in three *isolated* wetlands without a federal permit, the Army Corps of Engineers sought and won criminal and civil penalties against them. In *Rapanos v. U.S.*, the justices, in a flash of sanity, vacated the judgments and remanded the case. The Court quite sensibly defined "navigable waters" under the Clean Water Act as those of an interstate character.

But the ruling is apparently no obstacle for the ambitions of Messrs. Oberstar and Feingold. Their legislation established the authority of the Environmental Protection Agency over private ponds, ditches, wetlands, lakes—even dry stream beds that are infrequently wet and have no navigable function across state boundaries. Fearing a veritable wetlands *gestapo*, a number of groups, including the American Farm Bureau, are fighting the measure that redefines the Clean Water Act to include "intrastate waters" that would now be subject to the "legislative power of Congress under the Constitution."[48]

All of this represents a shocking expansion of central power. As Justice Clarence Thomas said sixty-three years after the *Wickard* decision in dissent over a homegrown medical marijuana case, "If Congress can regulate this under the Commerce Clause, then it can regulate virtually anything, and the federal government is no longer one of limited and enumerated powers."[49]

And so it is.

CHAPTER 6 NOTES

1. Stephan Dinan, "Health bill faces constitutional challenge," *The Washington Times*, 23 December, 2009.

2. http://reason .com/blog/2010/06/30/is-it-constitutional-well-its, (Accessed July 2010)

3. Ariane de Vogue, Devin Dwyer, "States Launch Legal Challenge to Health Care Law," *ABC News*, 23 March 2010. (Accessed March 2010)

4. *United States v. Lopez*, 514 U.S. (1995). In the *Lopez* case, the Supreme Court struck down the federal Gun Free Schools Zone Act of 1990 with the majority holding the "Act exceeds the authority of Congress "to regulate Commerce...among the several states" and said that the federal nexus for such interference ought to be "commerce which concerns more states than one."

5. Ariane de Vogue and Devin Dwyer, "States Launch Legal Challenge to Health Care Law," *ABC News,* 23 March 2010.

6. President Barack Obama interview with Jake Tapper, *ABC News*, 9 November 2009.

7. Amendment XVIII, United States Constitution, ratified 16 January 1919.

8. See Article 1, Section 8, United States Constitution, 1787.

9. Mortimer J. Adler, *We Hold These Truths* (New York: Collier Macmillan Publishers, 1987), 118.

10. Ibid., 119.

11. Thomas Jefferson, 15 Feb. 1791,*The Papers of Thomas Jefferson (Papers 19:275—80)* Edited by Julian P. Boyd, et al. (Princeton: Princeton University Press, 1950) http://press-pubs.uchicago.edu/founders/documents/a1_8_18s10.html., (Accessed January 2010)

12. Madison, "Federalist 41," *The Federalist Papers*, 222, 223.

13. Banning, *The Sacred Fire,* 326. Revisionists have argued that the nationalist sentiments of Madison, Jay, et al, were more influential than the anti-federalist fears of Patrick Henry and George Mason. But the gulf between the two parties has always been somewhat overblown. The real schism, as McDonald explains, originated with Madison's concern that the "national government be appropriately balanced and checked and refined, lest it become an engine of tyranny. The difference between him and Hamilton in this respect was evident even during the convention and even as they were cooperating in the writing of the Federalist." McDonald, *Novus Ordo,* 204-205.

14. Ronald J. Pestritto, "Theodore Roosevelt Was No Conservative," *The Wall Street Journal*, 27 December 2008. TR's reference to Thomas Paine as a "filthy little atheist" probably reveals more about Roosevelt than the Father of American Independence, considering that according to President John Adams, "Without the pen of Paine, the sword of Washington would have been wielded in vain," Charles Adams, *Those Dirty Rotten Taxes* (New York: The Free Press, 1998) 24.

15. Bork, *The Tempting of America.*

16. Michael S. Greve, "How to Think About Constitutional Change," *American Enterprise Institute*, June 2005.

17. *United States v. Butler*, 297 U.S. 1 1936.

18. Ibid.

19. Jack M. Balkin, "The Constitutionality of the Individual Mandate for Health Insurance, *The New England Journal of Medicine*, 14 January 2010

20. Ibid.

21. *South Dakota v. Dole*, 483 U.S. 203 (1987).

22. U.S. Census Bureau, *2010 U.S. Statistical Abstract*, Washington D.C.

23. Veronique de Rugy, "The Death of Fiscal Federalism," *Reason*, April 2010, 18.

24. Ibid.

25. Garner, *Black's Law Dictionary*. A "bill of attainder" amounts to a "legislative act prescribing capital punishment without a trial."

26. Ronald Reagan, "A Time for Choosing," Nationally televised address on behalf of Barry Goldwater's presidential campaign: 27 October 1964.

27. Richard Brookhiser, *Founding Father, Rediscovering George Washington* (New York: The Free Press, 1996) 55. Since altering the Articles required the consent of Congress as well as the state legislatures, initially, at the least, "the proposed convention was illegal," and Rhode Island never did send a delegation.

28. Banning, *The Sacred Fire,* 118.

29. Ibid., 53.

30. Ibid., 117.

31. Lineberry, et al, *Government in America,* 56. Of course, the Virginia Plan as Madison and Edmund Randolph envisioned merged with the so-called New Jersey Plan in the Connecticut Compromise that created a bicameral Congress based on population *and* state sovereignty, but leaving out any Congressional veto over state law.

32. Ibid., 48, 55. On this point, Madison thought "the interests of the states... meet in more points than they differ" and of course the Constitution delegates to Congress the ability to "regulate Commerce with foreign nations, and among the several states..."

33. Epstein, *How Progressive,* 33, 40 (quote), 41, 42. Epstein says that Justice Marshall's opinion in the controlling case of *Gibbons v. Ogden* (1824) was more about federal control over interstate commerce as in foreign commerce, not necessarily free trade. He and such organizations as the Cato Institute and the Institute for Justice are leading critics of an expansive state police power. Warning of the "danger of state monopolies," Epstein chides Brandeis' rationale for state experimentation as threatening to property rights, yet goes on to defend a federal rationale for antitrust enforcement—an anathema, as he acknowledges, to many libertarians. It is curious that critics of states' rights seem to fear local and state government monopolies, while at the same time endorsing national ones.

34. *United States v. Carolene Products Co.* 304 U.S. 144 (1938): 152, footnote 4. The Court upheld a federal law dictating the kinds of milk shipped in "interstate commerce."

35. *A.L.A. Schechter Poultry Corp. v. United States*, 295 U.S. 495 (1935).

36. Epstein, *How Progressives,* 64.

37. Amity Shales, *The Forgotten Man* (New York: Harper Collins, 2007) 204.

38. Ibid., 242.

39. Janice Rogers Brown, "A Whiter Shade of Pale," Speech to the Federalist Society, University of Chicago Law School, 20 April 2000.

40. *West Coast Hotel Co. v. Parrish* 300 U.S. 379 (1937).

41. *United States v. Darby*, 312, U.S. 100 (1941).

42. Ibid.

43. *United States v. Wrightwood Dairy Co.*, 315 U.S. 110 (1942).

44. *Wickard v. Filburn*, 317 U.S. 111 (1942). The Court's declaration that the government may "regulate that which it subsidizes" begs the question that a federal appropriation licenses the government to move beyond its enumerated powers? Which, of course, it does not.

45. Epstein, *How Progressives,* 48, 78.

46. Berger, *The Fourteenth Amendment,* 50.

47. *Rapanos v. United States 547 U.S. 715 (2006).* Similarly, a federal judge struck down President Obama's six-month drilling moratorium after the BP gulf oil spill in 2010 due in part to a lack of delegated authority by Congress to the Department of Interior.

48. See the Clean Water Restoration Act, HR 1356, Section 4, House of Representatives, 110 Congress of the United States.

49. *Gonzales v. Raich*, 545 U.S.1 (2005) 1, 8. In *Raich*, the Controlled Substances Act criminalized both interstate and intrastate commercial activity. Thomas noted his previous concurrence, *Lopez*, arguing that "allowing Congress to regulate intrastate, noncommercial activity under the Commerce Clause would confer on Congress a general police power over the nation."

CHAPTER 7

The Last Resort

WASHINGTON IS ON A ROLL. The biggest and most intrusive federal government the country has ever seen is now regulating the largest of institutions on Wall Street and the smallest on Main Street. The politicians authorized $700 billion to "save" the economy and the Federal Reserve doubled its balance sheet to two trillion dollars in the name of easy money. Detroit's automakers are a wholly owned subsidiary of federal bureaucrats and "the U.S. government, directly or indirectly, underwrites nine of every ten new residential mortgages..."[1] If that weren't enough, government-run healthcare is on the way.

The result? Our national debt is now approaching 100

percent of the gross domestic product; taxes and interest are set to rise once again; and the U.S. dollar is threatened with devaluation. Let's be frank; a nation that rations healthcare and energy; taxes work, savings and enterprise; and bankrupts it citizens and controls their property does not have the moral authority to instruct them on much of anything. But as bad as all this is, just what is to keep the Feds from devouring even more of our liberty? The answer, as we have seen, appears to be: not much.

What would happen, however, if citizens chose not to be governed in such a way? More to the point, what would be the outcome should a state actually desire to peaceably leave the Union? Since the Civil War established central power over the several states, is secession even possible? Would the federal government allow it, or would it declare war on that state? I have come to believe it should not, and that the notion of the United States as a voluntary compact be restored.

Theoretically, there are other solutions to omnipotent government than the threat of secession. The most preferable of which would include some sort of constitutional epiphany that results in Washington reining itself in. That, however, seems unlikely. Two liberal members of the Supreme Court have retired during President Obama's first term; there seems little doubt the successors will be as equally enamored with federal power. Especially so considering that the other branches of government, those who might rein in the Court, have now taken it upon themselves to address every perceived problem, no matter how small, from sea to shining sea.

To wit: Congress is now debating whether NCAA Division 1 football teams should conclude their season with a playoff or a bowl game.[2] Politicians who see themselves fit to govern the Bowl Championship Series are probably the least likely body to protect the populace from the "supposed dangers of judiciary encroachment."[3]

In fact, legislators have only sporadically used their constitutional power under Article III, Sections 1 and 2, to remove appellate jurisdiction from the federal courts.[4] While conservative members have proposed protecting the Pledge of Allegiance as well as traditional marriage from appellate review, the danger here lies in giving Congress a green light to expand its own power. Besides, the Supreme Court could simply ignore any Congressional language aimed at curbing their power (just as it has done in recent cases involving the detention of unlawful enemy combatants).[5]

A more credible Congress could legitimately impeach

wayward judges as a way to control judicial activism, but that too seems unlikely in an era of judicial supremacy. After his failure to remove Samuel Chase from the bench, Jefferson himself called impeachment a "farce" and "not even a scarecrow."[6] And this was long before the modern legislator's appetite for abdicating responsibility by deliberately deferring the toughest political disputes to the courts through vaguely worded legislation.

The Americans with Disabilities Act is a perfect example. Businesses, under the law, are now forced to make a "reasonable accommodation," whatever that is. Some interpretations are so absurd (some golfers get "court imposed" motorized carts on the PGA Tour, and patrons in wheelchairs at strip clubs have demanded accommodations for lap dances) that the Supreme Court took four cases in 2002 to clarify and define just what the statute meant.[7] Congress in effect created a new standing to sue without ever defining it. Given such legislative ambiguity, judges no longer feel the need to be "guided by the laws passed by Congress and the state legislatures," but by their own policy preferences.[8] This hardly squares with the Hamiltonian idea of a judiciary that would be "beyond comparison the weakest of the three department(s) of power."[9]

Perhaps all that is needed is a modern-day Andrew Jackson willing to defy the Supreme Court (as well as veto extra-constitutional legislation). The combative seventh president once said of the chief justice of the United States, "John Marshall has made his decision, now let him enforce it."[10] In those days, the Court wasn't looked upon as really establishing the "law of the land, but merely the law of the case."[11] Regardless, executive restraint seems quaint now that presidents of both major parties are more than eager to expand what the federal government may do: former president George W. Bush on education spending, Medicare entitlements, and bailouts;[12] President Obama on all of the above, plus a few trillion dollars more.

Other ideas for limiting federal power include judicial elections (which many states employ) instead of federal appointment or the requirement of a unanimous vote on questions of constitutionality. Graglia even suggests "a constitutional amendment simply abolishing judicial review."[13] That however fails to address legislative or executive ambition. The problem after all is not just the courts; it's the entire federal apparatus.

Some libertarians, on the other hand, seem willing to restrain the political branches, but not the courts (liberals apparently restrain nothing). Law professor Randy Barnett has proposed constitutional amendments to rein in legislative and executive power while maintaining judicial hegemony to uphold "any enumerated or unremunerated right, privilege or immunity" recognized by the Fourteenth Amendment.[14] Epstein praises the Court for striking down a state law that had prohibited instruction in a foreign language to any student who had not completed the eighth grade.[15] He chides Justice Oliver Wendell Holmes dissent, which said the Constitution simply doesn't prevent this experiment of encouraging a common language. Though the law certainly appeared heavy-handed as it pertained to private schools, one is still left to wonder the fate of more reasoned requirements in the public sphere (such as English Only laws that a number of states have passed) in the sort of legal paradigm Epstein envisions.

State bureaucracies can no doubt be quite oppressive. But why would any self-respecting skeptic of big government be willing to trade the vagaries of state government for the omnipotence of national rule?[16] At the very least, local citizens enjoy a distinct advantage by having political power limited by a much smaller geographic boundary. I suppose it's somewhat intoxicating to imagine the federal courts as the one great arbiter of freedom. But the courts have proven themselves incapable of protecting some of our most basic liberties. Moreover, they seem quite willing to stand by while a federal Leviathan devours the rest.

Of course, were "enlightened statesmen" to appoint all the justices and run all the departments of government, none should fear for their freedoms.[17] That has never been the case, so the only assurance to guard against imperfect rulers is the republican model. In other words, a process that checks runaway majority rule just as it does minority rule.

Freedom is best protected right at home. Frenchman Alexis de Tocqueville, in his nineteenth century classic *Democracy in America*, praised the virtue of the New England "township" as the cornerstone of "independence and power."[18] Jefferson's "ward republics" were best able, de Tocqueville wrote, "to scatter power in order to interest more people in public affairs."[19] As author Charles Murray later said, "legitimate functions of government should be performed at the most local feasible level" as "it is much easier for the average person to move out of Detroit than it is for him to move out of Michigan, and infinitely easier than to move out of the United States."[20]

It is in this context that Madison's vision of a "partly

national, partly federal" government is key—a vision that above all did not tell the states which programs to fund and which laws to pass.[21] "The proposed government cannot be deemed a national one," Madison opined, "since its jurisdiction extends to certain enumerated objects only, and leaves to the several states a residuary and inviolable sovereignty over all other objects."[22]

In September of 1787, when leaving the Constitutional Convention, Benjamin Franklin was reportedly asked by a local woman, "What kind of government have you given us, Dr. Franklin?" He answered, "A republic, madam, if you can keep it."[23] The best way to do so is by recognizing the limits of federal authority and deferring to the legislative or political branches of government in their respective jurisdictions. In fact, there's a greater case for dividing government along vertical lines than horizontal.[24] Only this character of our Constitution enables our republic to gently fall between the deficiencies of a monarchy on the one hand and unfettered democracy on the other.

About the only thing worse than a democratic majority without constitutional checks and balances is a government run by a minority without them. "The only way a republican government can function," Jefferson declared, "and the only way a people's voice can be expressed to effect a practicable control of government, is through a process in which decisions are made by the majority. This is not a perfect way of controlling government, but the alternatives—decisions made by a minority, one person—are even worse and are a source of great evil. To be just, majority decisions must be in the best interest of all the people, not just one faction,"[25]

A republic embraces majority rule, but only after thoughtful deliberation. The Electoral College, for example, provides for protection against large population centers by giving smaller states a substantial weighting in choosing the chief executive. The Senate accomplishes this through the idea of unlimited debate. When Vice-President Joe Biden demeaned the Senate filibuster, suggesting that "no democracy has survived needing a super majority," he displayed a startling ignorance on the crucial differences between republicanism and democracy, not to mention the long history of the filibuster.[26]

What the founders envisioned was a collection of states able to unite on a few national goals, but only when there was broad consensus. That is, small states held disproportionate power to veto legislation not in their interest by having the same number of senators as large states.[27] They were to remain masters of their own destiny in those areas of governance which lacked the support of a supermajority of citizens.

If that resulted in a minority—albeit a substantial one—holding up the wishes of a slim majority, so be it. National policy was not to be determined by a mere fifty-one percent—state sovereignty required much more. The American experiment has a wonderful bias against legislation by demanding a meeting of the minds before government can act.

State government used to employ the same checks and balances. But as law professor Stephen Presser lamented, "In the 1960s, the federal courts, guided by egalitarianism and emboldened by the triumph of Legal Realism, ordered that all state legislatures had to be redistricted solely on population, even though, for almost two centuries, many states had emulated the federal government's model and had an upper house of the legislature based on traditional political subdivisions."[28]

A republic, once again, is more than just a lack of kings and queens; it is governing philosophy that unites disparate interests by emphasizing local control "extended over a large region."[29] It is neither a monarchy nor a democracy, but as some have put it, a "filtered" majority refined with representation, and constrained by a constitutional separation of powers.[30] These constitutional guidelines serve to make our popular consultations much more deliberative and assured, but they do not render them impossible. Those who see the Constitution as only an anti-majoritarian document forget that it too is amended by the majority, albeit a super majority. In fact, all organized societies are, by default, either self-governed or tyrannical. "The choice," as Justice Jackson once reminded his colleagues, "is between liberty with order or anarchy without either," and the danger lies in converting "the constitutional Bill of Rights into a suicide pact" by forgetting they were crafted to limit central power, not aggrandize it.[31]

This is not to trust the mob, far from it. A representative republic is best suited to protect the rights of the individual because the federal government is prohibited from unconstitutional interference with the states, as are the states from one another. In other words, people are free to choose the laws under which they live. Only self-government allows for the people to change the law with free and open elections. And if they don't prefer the law in their state, they may leave. The most potent weapon that empowers self-government, while at the same time protecting the minority, is limited jurisdiction.

However, "If the courts are free to write the Constitution anew," as Justice Scalia warned, "they will write it the way the majority wants; the appointment and confirmation process will see to that. This, of course, is the end of the Bill of Rights, whose meaning will be committed to the very body it was meant to protect against: the majority."[32]

A division of governmental power is far better able to protect the rights of the individual—the greatest minority—than any federal authority could possibly hope to. The states themselves are bound by their own charters, legal precedent, and common law tradition.[33] Detractors of reinvigorating the states predictably warn of a return to Jim Crow, but that should be enough to make even a straw man blush.

No one disputes the federal prohibition on racial classifications through a proper reading of equal protection and due process in the Fourteenth Amendment. In other words, the right "to make and enforce contracts, to sue, be parties and give evidence, to inherit, purchase, lease, sell, hold, and convey real personal property and to full and equal benefit of all laws and proceedings for the security of person and property."[34] Restated: the same privileges and immunities that are awarded to all fellow citizens. But that remains a far cry from the federal government we have in the twenty-first century.

Most Americans understand that is time to return power to the states and for the federal government to rediscover its boundaries. Unfortunately, there remains enough confusion about the history surrounding the events described in this book to serve as a semblance for even more intrusion by big government. There are, it is true, contradictory statements from the authors of the Fourteenth Amendment. Rep. Bingham for instance, at times suggested that *Barron* should be overruled and the Bill of Rights enforced upon the states.[35]

But he also said, "The care of the property, the liberty, and the life of the citizen, under solemn sanction of an oath imposed by your Federal Constitution, is in the states and not in the federal government. I have sought to effect no change in that respect in the Constitution of the country."[36] These conflicting statements from Bingham or others were rarely countered because most legislators already understood the actual intent of the Amendment before they agreed to support it.[37]

Besides, "remarks of a particular proponent of the (Fourteenth) Amendment," as Justice Felix Frankfurter once put it, "no matter how influential, are not to be deemed part of the Amendment. What was submitted for ratification was his proposal, not his speech."[38]

Had it not been for the new state governments foisted upon the South under the Reconstruction Act of 1867, it's difficult to say whether the Fourteenth Amendment would even have been ratified. A number of states were apprehensive, and not just Southern ones; Ohio and New Jersey at one point threatened to withdraw their consent.[39] The Thirteenth Amendment abolishing slavery had been ratified by the "old" legislatures in 1865, but it took "new governments... under the direction of Congress" to ratify the Fourteenth.[40] Since the Thirteenth was never re-ratified by these approved legislatures, the result was such that one amendment or the other (depending on your preference) was passed by what Congress had considered an "unlawful" body.[41]

Regardless, it is now firmly embedded in the law. And in spite of everything written here (which means, in the author's opinion: in spite of the Constitution) we are nonetheless left with a century of Supreme Court jurisprudence that future justices seem unlikely to overturn. The Court has stretched the commerce clause; read all sorts of "penumbras" into the Ninth Amendment; and of course, firmly established its judicial hegemony through a revisionist reading of the "due process" clause. The genuine republican division of power as envisioned by the framers of the Constitution (as well as the authors of the Civil War Amendments) seems lost in a sea of legal ledger main.

We are left with is two competing visions of the republic. The one a federal compact envisioned by the Founding Fathers of a United States, and the other, transformed through war and judicial pretense into a would-be *United State*. I believe it is time to consider a new amendment to the Constitution: one that reclaims the origins of the republic and the Tenth Amendment by limiting all branches of the federal monolith. So I suggest a Twenty-Eighth Amendment to the United States Constitution with the following proposed language:

> Except where expressly stated, nothing in this Constitution or its Amendments shall grant to the executive, legislative, or judicial branch of the federal government jurisdiction over the several states.
>
> This prohibition of federal interference extends to but is not limited to all matters in the nature and substance of state legislation, providing such law affords its protection equally to all citizens and whose implementation is consistent with common law procedures of "due process."

The general welfare clause in the preamble and in Article 1, Section 8, of this Constitution shall not be construed to grant the federal branches of government any extended powers not previously or subsequently and specifically enumerated in this Constitution.

This Amendment also defines commerce among the states as only those economic transactions conducted between two or more states, and not those transactions conducted by parties or entities residing in the same state regardless of their impact upon commerce among the states. Furthermore, regulating commerce among the states may be used only to ensure the free flow of commercial transactions voluntarily established among the several states; it does not include the requirement or the elimination of economic transactions without further Amendments to this Constitution.

It is also hereby established that any state whose inhabitants desire through legal

means and in accordance with state law to
leave this union of the several states shall not
be forcibly refrained from doing so by the
federal government of these United States.

Uncomfortable as it may seem to some, this is not a
radical idea.[42] The states, under Article VII, voluntarily
ratified a Constitution of checks and balances in order to
preserve their independence. Jefferson's "wise and frugal
government which shall restrain men from injuring one
another" was to "leave them otherwise free to regulate
their own pursuits of industry and improvement."[43] And
notwithstanding Lincoln's noble wish of the "last best hope
of earth," the American idea was always more than a blind
allegiance to the nation-state.[44] It was a patriotism and belief
of the ideals behind it, including the notion of the voluntary
compact.

Limiting monopoly government returns the law to its
rightful place. Enlightenment philosopher John Locke put
forth the fundamental principle that "the end of law is not
to abolish or restrain but to preserve and enlarge freedom;
for in all states of created beings capable of laws, where there
is no law, there is no freedom. For liberty is to be free from

restraint and violence of others..."[45] He had also reasoned that no one born in "perfect freedom to order their actions and dispose of their possessions and persons as they think fit, within the bounds of nature..." would voluntarily give up his or her liberty for anything but self-government.[46] Hence, Jefferson's dictum that governments derive "their just powers from the Consent of the Governed..."[47]

No one argues for an unwise rush to secede. But there are no assurances that our governing class will ever abide by the limits of the Constitution. There must be an ultimate safety valve. If the voluntary compact were reestablished, merely the threat of secession would curb the appetites of federal power. According to DiLorenzo, had secession been an option before the Civil War, the "same reasons that led the colonists to form a Union in the first place would likely have become more appealing to both sections, and the Union would probably have been reunited."[48]

On the other hand, we know what happens to our blood and treasure when peaceful dissolution is forbidden. The British Constitution did not allow the colonies the option breaking free and the Civil War mindset categorized secession as rebellion.[49] The result was years of carnage, killing, and anarchy. President John F. Kennedy recalled in

1962 that "Those who make peaceful revolution impossible will make violent revolution inevitable."[50]

The truth is: there is little hope for a meaningful return to federalism as long as those who shape our political institutions are willing to use the power—military and otherwise—of the federal government as the ultimate deterrent.

Bastiat reminds us that "law is force, and that, consequently, the proper functions of law cannot lawfully extend beyond the proper function of force."[51] The legitimate task of government, therefore, is to prevent the *illegitimate* use of force (or fraud) by others. The state oversteps its bounds by using its monopoly on force to oppress, and that's why we limit its powers.[52] The paradox restated then "is to prevent people from doing through government that which they would do in the absence of government. The very purpose of constraints on government is the same as the purpose of government."[53]

It is here where the wisdom of original American thinking is most evident. By breaking up government, you limit its abuses, reclaim the balance of power, and entrust the people. Lord Acton, it seems, was right.[54] Power corrupts and absolute power corrupts absolutely. Is that not what the West proclaimed when Eastern Europe was struggling to break the yoke of Soviet bondage? How many times have we sided with those freedom fighters whose quest was liberation from centralized power? Hasn't that been America's message to the world for years? That no government is independent of the people.

Though it now appears unlikely you would find two-thirds of both Houses of Congress in support of relinquishing their own power by voting to amend the Constitution (according to Article V), the same number of state legislatures could. Given the number of states that have taken some action against Obamacare, a call for a constitutional convention is not beyond the realm of possibility. Indeed, just such a petition has passed the Florida senate and if approved by the house, it would represent "the twentieth state with an active call to do so."[55]

Of course, any amendment brought forth would still have to be ratified by "legislatures of three-fourths of the several states..."[56] But this nation is hopelessly divided on the most vexing issues of the day precisely because we ask the federal government to do too much—often against the will of our neighbors. If the nation were to coalesce around just a few tasks assigned to federal officials, we would heal many of our national wounds by letting people choose the law under which they live in their own state. That is the recipe for domestic tranquility.

In the final analysis, the American experiment is all about the principle of consent. Put another way: associations formed amongst a free people are to be voluntary. Hence, the right of secession is distinctly American. The belief that, should all else fail, the people retain the right to "dissolve the political bands which have connected them with another, and to assume among the Powers of Earth, the separate and equal station to which the Laws of Nature and of Nature's God entitle them..."[57]

CHAPTER 7 NOTES

1. Bob Davis, Deborah Soloman, and Jon Hilsenrath, "After the Bailouts, Washington's the Boss," *The Wall Street Journal*, 28 December 2009, A1.

2. http://sports.espn.go.com/ncf/news/story?id=4727426.(Accessed February 2010)

3. Hamilton, "Federalist 81," *The Federalist Papers*, 442.

4. Section III reads in part that "The judicial power of the United States shall be vested in one Supreme Court, and in such inferior courts as the Congress may from time to time ordain and establish." Section 2 allows the Supreme Court to have appellate jurisdiction, but "with such exceptions, and under such regulations as the Congress shall make." See *United States Constitution*, Article III, Section 1 & 2, Philadelphia, 1787.

5. *Hamden v. Rumsfeld*, 548 U.S. 557 (2006). In *Hamden*, the Court held that military tribunals set up by the Bush administration were unconstitutional despite the clear intent of Congress and the administration in the Detainee Treatment Act of 2005, which stated that "no court, justice, or judge shall have jurisdiction to hear...a writ of habeas corpus filed by or on behalf" of an illegal enemy alien held in Cuba.

6. Graglia, *Constitutional Law,* 7.

7. See *Barnes v. Gorman; Chevron v. Echazabal; US Airways v. Barnett; Toyota v. Williams.*

8. Brill, *The Court TV Cradle,* 413.

9. Hamilton, "Federalist 78," *The Federalist Papers*, 421.

10. Jon Meacham, *American Lion, Andrew Jackson in the White House* (New York: Random House, 2008) 204. The quote, attributed to Horace Greeley, is reflective of Jackson's rhetorical flourish, but in the end nothing much came of it, as the parties, in this case the state of Georgia and the Supreme Court, eventually found a solution. Jackson was also not shy about wielding federal force when he thought states were threatening the Union.

11. Manion, *Cancer in the Constitution*, 3.

12. Veronique de Rugy, "Bush's Regulatory Kiss-Off," *Reason*, January 2009, 25. de Rugy notes that the largest annual percentage increase in the total regulatory budget over the last fifty years occurred in during the George W. Bush administration. Bush defenders suggest it was primarily due to the war on terror, with new departments as the Homeland Security and the Transportation Security Administration.

13. Graglia, *Constitutional Law,* 51, 52.

14. Randy E. Barnett, "The Case for a Federalism Amendment," *The Wall Street Journal*, 23 April 2009 (Accessed May 2010)

15. Epstein, *How Progressives,* 103, 104. See *Meyer v. Nebraska* (1923).

16. Former Arkansas Governor Mike Huckabee actually proposed a federal smoking ban during the 2008 presidential primaries. Regardless of your view on tobacco, this is dangerous precedent.

17. See James Madison, "Federalist 10,"*The Federalist Papers*, 48.

18. Paul Anthony Rahe, *Soft Despotism, Democracy's Drift* (New Haven: Yale University Press, 2009) 199, 200.

19. Ibid.

20. Charles Murray, *What It Means To Be A Libertarian*, (New York: Broadway Books, 1997) 42, 43. The only constitutional difference is that federalism as the founders envisioned was a collection of states, not municipalities.

21. Madison, "Federalist 39," *The Federalist Papers*, 207.

22. Ibid.

23. Papers of Dr. James McHenry on the Federal Convention of 1787, in Charles C. Tansill, comp. *Documents Illustrative of the Formation of the Union of the American States* (Washington: U.S. Printing Office, 1927) 952.

24. The notion of coequal branches of government, taught in everyday civics, is actually a departure from the Founding Fathers who believed in legislative superiority, especially the House of Representatives, as Madison put it in "Federalist 58," *The Federalist Papers*.

25. Thomas Jefferson, (Charlottesville (VA): University of Virginia Library, Electronic Text Center; 1995; c1999 http://etext.lib.virginia.edu/jefferson/quotations/index. html. (Accessed May 2002)

26. Peter Roff, "Joe Biden's Filibuster Hypocrisy," *U.S. News & World Report*, 19 January 2010.

27. The passage of the Seventeenth Amendment in 1913, requiring the direct election of U.S. senators, instead of appointment by state legislature, severely weakened that body's ability to preserve the interest of the several states and counter the passions of the majority as represented in the House of Representatives.

28. Stephen B. Presser, "Sisyphus and States' Rights," *Chronicles*, April 1999, 13. Presser is talking about the "one man, one vote" rule of *Baker v. Carr* that so many liberals laud, even though it actually weakens minority rights by making the upper house reflect the majoritarian passions of the lower.

29. Madison, "Federalist 14," 69.

30. Benno Schmidt, et al, "James Madison" The notion of a "filtered" democracy has been attributed to Ellis, though it's hard to imagine such a generic description hasn't been used elsewhere to characterize the nuances of a Madisonian republic.

31. *Terminiello v. Chicago*, 337 U.S. 1 (1949).

32. Antonin Scalia, "Vigilante Justice," *National Review*, 10 February 1997, 35.

33. *Adamson v. California*, 332 U.S. 46 (1947). In *Adamson v. California*, while surprising for the day, the high court refused to apply the Fifth Amendment in its entirety to a state trial, leaving the decision to the states and common law.

34. Berger, *The Fourteenth Amendment*, 24, 25. Such was the language of the Civil Rights Act of 1870 enacted after the Fourteenth Amendment. There are also specific constitutional provisions prohibiting the states from "impairing the obligation of contracts," and the Constitution reserves bankruptcy law for the federal government so as to avoid providing unwarranted relief to debtors. See Article 1, Section 10 of U.S. Constitution [1787].

35. Amar and Adams, *The Bill*, 207, 208, 212, 213.

36. Berger, *The Fourteenth Amendment*, 30.

37. Ibid, 25, 26, 28, 29. While Bingham spoke eloquently about protecting via national law "the privileges and immunities of all the citizens" from "unconstitutional acts by the states," he was, according to Berger, more than just inconsistent. He at one point condemned federal oppression of the states and the next talked about advancing the protections of the Bill of Rights—all in the same speech. In fact, his muddled thinking on the matter prompted Stevens, another member of the committee hearing the civil rights bill, to say of Bingham, "In all this contest about reconstruction, I do not propose either to take his counsel, recognize his authority, or believe a word he says." Shankman and Pilon, "Reviving the Privileges," 20, 21.

38. Manion, *Cancer in the Constitution*, 24, 25. Frankfurter's concurring opinion in *Adamson*.

39. Ibid., 8.

40. Ibid., 8, 9. Quoting the Supreme Court's analysis in *Coleman v. Miller* in 1939.

41. Ibid., 8, 9, 10.

42. Commentary, *Crusade Magazine*, November/December 2009. The religious principle of "subsidiarity" is nothing new, stemming "from the fact that man is not only a social being but also a rational, essentially free and responsible being. Thus he is guaranteed the right to resolve his problems either by himself, through his family, or other intermediate social bodies without being obliged to wait for solutions from public authority"

43. Rozwenc, *The Making,* 278.

44. America as the "last best hope of earth" is from Lincoln's *Annual Message to Congress,* 1 December 1862.

45. John Locke, *The Second Treatise of Government,* 1690, edited by Thomas Peardon, (Macmillan, 1952) 32.

46. Ibid. Natural law suggests a code discoverable by human reason that society must observe for civilization to flourish. Modern-day philosophers such as Ayn Rand have further developed their own rational case for liberty.

47. See the Declaration of Independence, Philadelphia, 1776.

48. DiLorenzo, *The Real Lincoln,* 272.

49. Jaffa, *A New Birth,* 191. Jaffa, a Lincoln biographer, notes that the British Constitution "did not admit a right of secession" as did the Articles of Confederation. Jaffa, however, supports the idea that the American Constitution treats attempts to leave the Union as "rebellion" because there "could hardly be a justification for secession under the Constitution."

50. JFK at White House speech, 1962. http://www.quotationspage.com/quote/24966.html. (Accessed April 2010)

51. Bastiat, *The Law,* 28.

52. Otto Scott, "Back to the Future," *International Money & Politics*, Nov/Dec. 1993, 12. Some have even pondered taking government out of the picture completely, suggesting no such thing as a "public good," but only private rights. In this scenario, existing before positive law, those who refused to abide by the decisions of voluntary tribunals would be "banished from the tribe." "Outlawry" became a system where a perpetrator's person and property were "outside the protection of the law" and victims could take their own recourse without recrimination. Hence, the term "outlaw."

53. Dwight R. Lee and Richard B. McKenzie, *Regulating Government* (Lexington: Lexington Books Inc., 1987) 8.

54. DiLorenzo, *The Real Lincoln*, 267. Acton had actually favored the right of secession and wrote a letter to that effect to General Robert E. Lee once the South was vanquished. "I saw in states' rights the only availing check upon the absolutism of sovereign will, and secession filled me with hope... as the redemption of Democracy," wrote the famed English historian.

55. James M. Lemunyon, "A Constitutional Convention Can Rein In Washington," *The Wall Street Journal*, 31 March 2010.

56. See Article V, *United States Constitution*, Philadelphia, 1787.

57. See *Declaration of Independence*, Philadelphia, 1776.

KEY DATES

This lists important moments discussed in the text, and is not intended to include all the decisions that the high court has made.

September 5, 1774—Continental Congress meets for the first time.

July 4, 1776—Declaration of Independence is officially signed in Philadelphia.

March 1, 1781—Articles of Confederation are ratified.

September 3, 1783—Treaty of Paris is signed declaring the thirteen colonies as free and sovereign states.

May 25, 1787—Constitutional Convention opens in order to revise the Articles of Confederation.

September 17, 1787—U.S. Constitution is adopted at the Constitutional Convention in Philadelphia.

March 4, 1789—First Congress meets as the U.S. Constitution goes into effect.

June 8, 1789—James Madison introduces the Bill of Rights in Congress.

December 15, 1791—Bill of Rights is ratified.

February 16, 1833—Justice John Marshall says the Bill of Rights applies only to the federal government in *Barron v. Baltimore*.

December 20, 1860—South Carolina formally secedes from the United States of America.

March 4, 1861—Lincoln declares that the Union is perpetual in his first inaugural.

July 9, 1868—Fourteenth Amendment to the Constitution is ratified.

April 14, 1873—Supreme Court warns in *Slaughter-House* cases against the federal judiciary becoming a perpetual censor on the states.

October 15, 1883—*Civil Rights* cases declare that Fourteenth Amendment prohibits discrimination by state governments only.

April 8, 1913—Seventeenth Amendment is ratified requiring the direct election of U.S. senators.

June 8, 1925—Supreme Court in *Gitlow v. New York* says the due process clause of the Fourteenth Amendment protects "fundamental" rights from impairment by state legislatures.

April 25, 1938—In *U.S. v. Carolene Products* the Supreme Court rejects the notion that property rights are "fundamental," giving greater scrutiny to what they would describe as "discrete and insular minorities."

November 9, 1942—Supreme Court ruling in *Wickard v. Filburn* establishes that those intrastate activities that merely affect interstate commerce are subject to federal regulation.

September 25, 1962—U.S. Senate confirms Arthur Goldberg's nomination to the Supreme Court, thus beginning the heyday of the Warren Court. Though the Court had already started its descent into settling "political questions" with its ruling on legislative reapportionment, what followed with a liberal 5-4 majority was a series of controversial decisions involving everything from prayer to privacy. Warren's legacy remains the foundation for much of the modern Court's activism.

SUGGESTED READINGS AND OTHER RESOURCES

Adler, Mortimer J., *We Hold These Truths* (New York: Collier Macmillan Publishers, 1987).

Banning, Lance, *The Sacred Fire of Liberty: James Madison and the Founding of the Federal Republic* (Ithaca: Cornell University Press, 1995).

Bastiat, Frederic, *The Law,* 1848 (Whittier: reprinted by Constructive Action, Inc., 1964).

Berger, Raoul, *The Fourteenth Amendment and the Bill of Rights,* (Norman: University of Oklahoma, 1989).

Bork, Robert H., *The Tempting of America* (New York: The Free Press, 1990).

Bowen, Tucker, "Lincoln: American Mastermind," National Geographic Television, 2009.

Boyd, Julian P., ed., *The Papers of Thomas Jefferson* (Princeton: Princeton University Press, 1950) http://press-pubs.uchicago.edu/founders/documents/a1_8_18s10.html.

Brookhiser, Richard, *Founding Father, Rediscovering George Washington* (New York: The Free Press, 1996).

Brown, Janice Rogers, "A Whiter Shade of Pale," Speech to the Federalist Society, University of Chicago Law School, 20 April 2000.

Cavanaugh, Tim, "Ninth Configurations," *Reason*, February 2010.

Chadwick, Michael L., ed., *The Federalist Papers* (Washington: Global Affairs Publishing Co., 1987).

Cramer, Clayton E., *For the Defense of Themselves and the State: The Original Intent and Judicial Interpretation of the Right to Keep and Bear Arms* (Westport: Praeger, 1994).

de Rugy, Veronique, "The Death of Fiscal Federalism," *Reason*, April 2010.

DiLorenzo, Thomas J., *The Real Lincoln* (Roseville: Prima Publishing, 2002).

Ellen, Paul, "Taking Liberty," *Reason*, March 1984.

Ellis, Joseph, *Founding Brothers*, (New York: Alfred Knopf, 2000).

Epstein, Richard, *How Progressives Rewrote the Constitution* (Washington: Cato Institute 2006).

Graglia, Lino A., *Constitutional Law without the Constitution: The Supreme Court's Remaking of America* (Stanford: Hoover Institution Press, 2005).

Greve, Michael S., "How to Think About Constitutional Change," American Enterprise Institute, June 2005.

Huber, Peter, *Liability: The Legal Revolution and Its Consequences* (New York: Basic Books, 1988).

Jefferson, Thomas, (Charlottesville (VA): University of Virginia Library, Electronic Text Center; 1995; c1999) http://etext.lib.virginia.edu/jefferson/quotations/index.html.

Kopff, E. Christian, *The Devil Knows Latin: Why American Needs the Classical Tradition*, (Wilmington: ISI Books, 2001).

Lash, Kurt T., *The Lost History of the Ninth Amendment* (New York: Oxford, 2009).

Lee, Dwight R., and McKenzie, Richard B., *Regulating Government* (Lexington: Lexington Books, Inc., 1987).

Levy, Robert A., and Mellor, William, *The Dirty Dozen* (New York: Sentinel Publishing, 2008).

Locke, John, *The Second Treatise of Government*, 1690, edited by Thomas Peardon, (Macmillan, 1952).

Manion, Clarence, *Cancer in the Constitution* (Shepherdsville: Victor Publishing Co., 1972).

Maybury, Richard J., *Whatever Happened to Justice?* (Placerville: Bluestocking Press, 1993).

McDonald, Forrest, *Novus Ordo Seclorum* (Lawrence: University Press of Kansas, 1985).

————, *States' Rights and the Union*, (Lawrence: University Press of Kansas, 2000).

Murray, Charles A., *What It Means To Be A Libertarian*, (New York: Broadway Books, 1997).

Presser, Stephen B., "Sisyphus and States' Rights," *Chronicles*, April 1999.

Rehnquist, William, dissent in *Roe v Wade*, 410 U.S. 113 (1973).

Ring, Kevin, ed., *Scalia Dissents* (Washington: Regnery Publishing, 2004).

Scalia, Antonin, majority opinion in *Dist. of Columbia v. Heller*, 554 U.S. ___ (2008).

Schmidt, Benno; Ellis, Joseph; and Wilentz, Sean, C-SPAN, "James Madison and the Constitution," New York Historical Society Panel Discussion, October 2, 2008. www.c-spanvideo.org/program/281562-1

Scott, Otto, "Back to the Future," *International Money & Politics*, Nov/Dec. 1993.

Shales, Amity, *The Forgotten Man* (New York: Harper Collins, 2007).

Smith, Edward Conrad, *The Constitution of the United States with Case Summaries*, Tenth Edition, (New York: Harper Row, 1975).

Sobran, Joseph, "Restore the Constitution," *Chronicles*, October 2000.

Spooner, Lysander, *An Essay on the Trial by Jury*, www.barefootsworld.net/trial01.html, 1852.

Tansill, Charles C., ed., Papers of Dr. James McHenry on the Federal Convention of 1787, *Documents Illustrative of the Formation of the Union of the American States* (Washington: U.S. Printing Office, 1927).

The Constitution of the United States (1787).

The Declaration of Independence (1776).

Thomas, Clarence, dissenting opinion in *Gonzales v. Raich*, 545 U.S. 1 (2005).

Tribe, Lawrence, *Abortion: The Clash of Absolutes*, (New York: W.W. Norton, 1990).

Winik, Jay, *April 1865* (New York: Harper Collins, 2001).

ABOUT THE AUTHOR

KNOWN AS "AMERICA'S MR. RIGHT," Jason Lewis is a radio talk show host and political commentator whose weekday program the *Jason Lewis Show* is nationally syndicated on Premiere Radio Networks. Lewis began his radio career at KOA in Denver and has hosted local talk shows at WBT-AM Charlotte, and KTLK-FM as well as KSTP-AM in Minneapolis/St. Paul, where he was rated number one.

Lewis was selected as one of the top twenty-five talk hosts in the country by *Newsmax Magazine* and has been twice featured in ABC Radio's "The Year in Talk." While in Charlotte he was named one of "The Heavy Hundred" most important talk show hosts in the nation by *Talkers Magazine*, a talk radio trade magazine.

Lewis has been quoted in the *Washington Post* and has

written editorials for newspapers throughout the country, including the *Wall Street Journal*. He has appeared on NBC's *Today Show*, Fox News Channel, CNN, CNBC, and MSNBC.

Lewis has a master's degree in political science from the University of Colorado-Denver and a bachelor's degree in education/business from the University of Northern Iowa. In 1990, Lewis was the Republican nominee for the United States Congress from Colorado's Second Congressional District.

He lives with his wife and two daughters in Minnesota.

www.jasonlewisshow.com